The Beloved Disciple

His Name · His Story · His Thought

Two Studies

from th...

VER

Willia...

Grand...

Library of Congress Cataloging-in-Publication Data

Eller, Vernard.
   The beloved disciple — his name, his story, his thought : two
studies from the Gospel of John / Vernard Eller.
   p.   cm.
   ISBN 0-8028-0275-3
   1. Bible. N.T. John — Criticism, interpretation, etc. 2. Bible.
N.T. John — Authorship. 3. Bible. N.T. John — Theology.
4. John, the Apostle, Saint.   5. Lazarus, of Bethany, Saint.
6. Sacraments — Biblical teaching. I. Title.
BS2615.2.E44   1987   87-16772
226'.506 — dc19   CIP

Contents

Preface

There is no way the matter could have been kept secret, yet very few people know that the Gospel we call "of John" neither names nor gives any action to the "John" whom the Gospel presumably is "of." The one and only verse coming anywhere close is verse 2 of chapter 21. It lists the seven followers of Jesus who were present at his resurrection-appearance on the seashore, and includes "the sons of Zebedee."

No one named "John" is to be found (excepting "John the Baptist," of course)—yet the Gospel is quite explicit about just who is the source of its information (and in that sense the *author* of the work). It is "the disciple whom Jesus loved," whom we hereafter will refer to as "the Beloved Disciple." And it is this person who now is to be the subject of our study as we set out to discover his name, his story, and his thought. In order to keep us from jumping to conclusions before we have seen any evidence, I will always call him "the Beloved Disciple" (never "John") and always call his Gospel "The Fourth Gospel" (never "The Gospel of John").

In time, we will come through on our promise to name him by name, tell his story, and expound his thought—though it will take us a goodly while to get to that point. However, Messrs. Eller and Eerdmans (as good a title for the two as anyone has come up with) will take it very badly if readers start turning immediately to the back of the book in an effort to get at the answers. The intent and purpose of this book is not particularly to arrive at those answers but to conduct a *study* which, in the process of getting to those answers, can afford us much good biblical education. The Sherlockian solving of the Mystery of

the Beloved Disciple is only a "come-on." So the response now
expected is that you "come on"—without cheating.

Whether this book be read by an individual or used as the
basis for a group study (it should work either way), the hope is
that things will proceed step by careful step—the very way Mr.
S. Holmes used to build his cases. You will need at least a New
Testament (pick your version; I am using the RSV, although
without prejudice toward any other version)—and a pipe,
magnifying glass, and deerstalker hat only if you like "atmo-
sphere." If they happen to be available, a "parallel of the Gospels" and a concordance might also prove handy.

Particularly in the early going, the "old pros" from among
us Bible students can breeze along at a great rate—it will be old
stuff to them. At the same time, the "rank beginners" better
plan on putting one slow foot after another, taking time to look
up the Scripture references and check that they actually do say
what I say they say. This ought not be tedious. The case is,
rather, that you will be encountering new ideas ("I never knew
that before!"), ideas which will take a little digesting and getting
used to. "Learning Bible" will begin with page 1, instead of
coming all at once with the way-down-the-line naming of the
Beloved Disciple. (For a starter, you have already learned that
the Gospel of John never names its supposed author—John
the son of Zebedee—haven't you? And that fact you can check
out by reading the entire Gospel through on your own.)

A number of pretty fair Bible scholars already have expressed the opinion that this present book is reputable, helpful, and interesting. However, that does not mean it is "scholarly" in the customary sense of the term. My own hope is that it
can be scholarly without being scholarly—its "unscholarliness"
lying in the fact that I never make any effort to consult authorities, collect learned opinions, or enlist outside experts to
bolster one point or another. Understand, it's not that I have
anything against this *modus operandi;* it's simply that I have
chosen not to employ the method here. In the *reviewing* of the
book is where the "scholars" will have a chance to get even for
my having ignored them.

But here I'm going all the way with Sherlock himself—namely, working the case entirely from "internal evidence," fathoming the truth simply from the clues at hand. Did Holmes ever have to resort to help from outside experts? Of course not, and no more will we. We can crack this thing with just what the New Testament and particularly the Fourth Gospel can tell us about themselves, with just what the Beloved Disciple tells us about himself. And the big advantage, of course, is that this puts all of us on the very same footing—the old pro, the rank beginner, any reader of the book whatsoever. Each of us has the same access to every clue (all the data). All we have to do is figure out what these clues mean.

This book consists of two separate studies—the first dealing more with the Beloved Disciple's identity and personal history, the second more with his theology. Each of the two studies came into being in a rather funny way (as with most of my stuff) and quite independent of the other. In fact, both had been complete for some time before I even caught on that they could go together to form a book. (I would suppose very few of you can appreciate what it must be like always to be writing without having any idea what you are doing.)

Yet, in the case of the first study, it is providential (I guess) that, in my spring-semester college class called "Introduction to the New Testament," our treatment of the Fourth Gospel always comes last, just before summer vacation. (Yes, I *do* know that Revelation comes last in the New Testament, thank you. But I'll teach things my way, if you don't mind.) Well, in that unit of study, a point I try most strongly to make is this: What simply will not do is to try to read the New Testament as though it presents *four* Gospels that pretty well parallel and support each other—each telling what is essentially the same story in essentially the same way, each complementing and filling in the others to produce what can be taken as *one* gospel account. That "confluencing" of the streams will work fairly well with the first *three* Gospels (the Synoptics), but making the Fourth Gospel flow in the same channel can be done only at great violence to the Gospel itself. It clearly was never meant to be so treated. If we are to make sense of it at all, we must deal with it as a self-contained entity in its own right.

Though in that class the end was upon us and the time all too short (as always), I did get the point well enough made for at least some students to pass the test. Yet, with the kids gone and me having nothing better to do, my somewhat absent-minded professorial brain kept right on teaching into the summer. It got an idea of how to let the respective texts show for themselves just how different the Fourth Gospel is from the Synoptics. I thought it might be smart to get some notes into black and white (actually my word processor does green on black) so I would have them when the Fourth Gospel came around again a year later. But wouldn't you know, before I could get away from that word processor (I was at it for the better part of a month), I had keyed in the very file that in time printed out as the text which, within a page or two, you will be reading. The only problem was that my "notes" were too substantial for an article and not substantial enough for a book and so had to be left on disk as a "neither." (I did use them in class the next year, however.)

I didn't even know that the second study was going to concern the Fourth Gospel. I was supposed to be writing something on the "sacraments" of the church, notably the Lord's Supper. And this particular piece had taken its impetus from a statement attributed to Karl Barth: "There is only *one* sacrament—the one who has himself risen from the dead." I, for one, felt it was nice of him to have said that, though I wasn't quite sure what he meant. Later on I learned that his son Markus had lectured on the "one sacrament" idea, using it to expound John 6. Well, I had earlier written on the antisacramentalism of John 6, so I knew where that chapter was.

Learning that there was a "one sacrament" idea in John 6 was all the help I got from the Barths, but that was enough. I started in, and (once more) one thing led to another until I was clear out in left field. My focus now was not just the Lord's

Supper—soon I was grappling with the whole character of religious experience and modern Christendom. My focus was no longer just John 6—soon I was involved with the whole of the Fourth Gospel and even the implications of the Beloved Disciple's being the author of it. And my focus had expanded to more than just one idea out of the Fourth Gospel—soon I had hold of what I am convinced the Beloved Disciple intended as his central theme.

When I realized that this second study could be paired with the first study to make a book, all in the world it took to turn the trick was a bit of playing down my original lead-in on Lord's Supper sacramentalism. As fate (or whoever) would have it, I had written a book on the Beloved Disciple's identity, personal history, and theological thought without once knowing what I was doing. If this is what is meant by writing under the inspiration of the Spirit, I sure wish the Spirit had seen fit to identify himself once in a while and let me know what was going on.

So how this book ever got itself written in the first place—that's one mystery. But the "who done it" of the Fourth Gospel—that mystery is the come-on. So, come on!

Study One

The Beloved Disciple: His Name and His Story

OPENING THE CASE (AS HOLMES WOULD)

The Problem

Before we can even begin to treat the Fourth Gospel (let alone the identity of the Beloved Disciple), we need to get a good bit of practice in handling simply the raw data that could come from any of the Gospels. Thus, a major hope for this study is that it might give the laity who have had but slight contact with biblical scholarship at least something of a feel for what Bible scholars are supposed to be about and *how* they do what they are supposed to be about. To the laity, this is probably a more unfathomable mystery than the identity of the Beloved Disciple. They honestly can't figure what Bible scholars could possibly be good for, and they must think that scholars pursuing their work are like psychics—super-intellectuated beings who read a passage of Scripture, close their eyes, "ponder" for an interval of minutes, hours, or days, and then open their eyes to declaim the very TRUTH OF GOD (in incomprehensible terms having no apparent connection with the Scripture just read). Now I admit I have seen studies that seem to have been done that very way, but such is not true biblical scholarship. Our case will demonstrate only one of the many methods scholars use, yet readers will find themselves (subconsciously, I hope) actually *being* scholars rather than just hearing reports from or rumors about them.

1

Further, I hope that readers (again, subconsciously) will come to sense the fundamental nature of the Gospel evidences with which we are dealing. By "Gospel evidences" I have in mind the historical data, the "factual knowledge bits" that come from any and all of the four Gospels in the form of names of individuals or places involved in the story; chronological hints about what happened before or after something else did; and accounts of what happened where, who did what, and who said what. The problem is that "people" on the one hand and "scholars" on the other are of two different minds regarding what those "factual knowledge bits" actually represent and how they properly are to be used.

"People" tend to assume that the collected "bits" from all four Gospels are jigsaw pieces that can be fitted together to form one complete and uniform puzzle picture. Once we get them properly arranged and related, these pieces will give us the one real, true, historically factual picture of Jesus and his career—an accurate *biography* of Jesus, if you will.

The difficulty is that the "scholars" (the professional puzzle-doers) cannot for the life of them use all the pieces and make them into the uniform puzzle picture that is supposed to result. Yes, many individual puzzle-doers *claim* to have the solution. The trouble is that no two of them come up with the same picture; each tends to produce the portrait of Jesus he had in mind before even starting work on the puzzle. It is apparent that these people subconsciously are selecting their pieces to *compose* a picture rather than *discovering* the one the puzzle supposedly embodies.

Scholars now generally agree that one root of the problem is the assumption that the one uniform puzzle picture can be produced without giving attention to the color of the *back* of the various pieces—that is, without paying attention to the source of any piece, whether it was originally a piece of Mark, of Matthew, of Luke, or of John. To mix together the pieces of *four* different puzzles and then to try to arrange them to form *one* picture probably was not the smartest way to go at jigsaw puzzling. Scholars have found that we will get farther by using "Mark pieces" to build a "Mark picture," "Matthew pieces" to build a "Matthew picture," and so forth—if we then can live with the fact that each of the Gospels presents a unique picture that will never completely jibe with the others.

Scholars also realize that, when anyone claims to have arranged *all* of the pieces to give us one complete puzzle picture, he inevitably has done (subconsciously, we assume) a certain amount of "fudging" (let's not call it "cheating"). I propose that this happens in three ways:

1. When confronted with some obstinate pieces that just cannot be made to fit anywhere, we tend to brush them surreptitiously off the table into the wastebasket—to conveniently overlook the existence of biblical evidence that disagrees with the evidence we have chosen to use at a given place.

2. With other pieces we simply snip off the "peninsulas" (or whatever those parts that stick out are called) that keep them from fitting where we think they belong. Again, we do a mental trimming and conveniently dispose of any details that don't quite fit the picture.

3. Conversely, we resort to using Silly Putty to add a needed peninsula to a piece that's too small, reshaping it until it *will* fit the hole we have in mind for it. This Silly Putty is what I call "pious imagination," our inventing something to explain a discrepancy and then treating the piece just as though it had come that way directly out of Scripture. For instance, the Fourth Gospel says that Peter was from Bethsaida, and the Synoptics say he was from Capernaum. Pious imagination takes care of the gap (a matter of less than five miles) by explaining that Peter, at some point, *moved* from Bethsaida to Capernaum. Of course, there is no textual evidence for that solution, yet there is a sort of mind that just *has* to have the matter settled, whereas the scholarly mind prefers to let the textual facts stand as they are, to accept the incongruity of the Fourth Gosepl's saying "Bethsaida" where the Synoptics say "Capernaum." What difference does it make which is histor-

ically accurate? Peter (perhaps living halfway between) undoubtedly was familiar with both towns.

However, if we *start* from the premise that, in order for the
Scriptures to be *Scripture,* it must be taken as certain that all the
pieces from all four Gospels *will* indeed fit together into one
factual puzzle picture of the history of Jesus—if we start from
this premise, then it is probably inevitable that, in our efforts to
force that picture, we will fall into "fudging." And this is precisely why the "scholars" therefore ask us to consider the possibility that we may be misunderstanding and misusing the
Gospel evidences in even *wanting* to jigsaw-puzzle them in such
a way.

What if it were the case that it had never even entered the
heads of the Gospel writers to give detailed, historically factual
accounts of the sort *we* think they should have given? We
would do well to remember that the passion for this sort of
journalistic factual accuracy is entirely an invention of modern
Western thought—about which peoples of the ancient world
knew nothing. What if the Gospel writers were careless about
such matters precisely because they could have cared less
about that sort of picture of Jesus, not seeing that it would be of
any particular Christian value to anyone? What if they knew—
knew better than we do—that their pieces didn't even pretend
to be journalistic "factual knowledge bits"? What if they knew
that what they actually were handling were rather "story units
of *tradition*" which had been passed along by word of mouth
and which the passers-along had freely molded and shaped to
give us the most *theologically* true interpretation of who Jesus
was and what he signifies as God's revelation to us? Could it be
that we have created the problem for ourselves in trying to
read the Gospels as one *historical* jigsaw puzzle when they were
meant to present us with a set of pictures of an entirely different sort?

Most people probably have never made the sort of detailed
comparison of the Gospels that reveals just how much discrepancy of detail there is between them. Accordingly, many are

likely to be shocked by what our study will now show to be the case. Some will even feel quite threatened—perhaps even resenting my bringing the truth to light.

In response, let me first of all point out that I am not *creating* these discrepancies; I am only pointing out what is in the texts. And of course, any student of Scripture will *want* to start with a totally honest acceptance of what the texts (*all* the texts) actually say.

Second, I will take pains to develop my view that these discrepancies in no way have the effect of challenging or questioning "the inspiration of Scripture." Rather, they afford us a very helpful means for discovering just how "the inspiration of Scripture" was understood by the Gospel writers themselves.

And third, we will find that it is precisely the *discrepancies* between the Gospels that give us our best clues regarding the respective authors—who each was, how each thought, and what each wanted to accomplish with his particular Gospel.

To help in our addressing these last two points, I shall lift up just one such Gospel discrepancy as an illustration. Because we are due to give it very detailed attention later, I will not now reveal as much as the chapter-verse locations. Please don't take the time to figure them out and look them up. The pro-and-con argument will come later; read what I say here as a simple illustration of the point I want to make. I also will be making some observations that will get supported only later. So, for now, don't argue—just read.

I have in mind the account of Jesus' original seashore calling of his Galilean fisherman disciples. Mark's Gospel is the one that has the best chance of being primary source material of precise historical accuracy. For one thing, Mark's account was written as much as twenty years before that of either Luke or Matthew. For another, there is the distinct possibility that Mark's account could have come straight from the mouth of Peter—who, of course, was himself one of the fishermen called. And for a third, the accounts of Luke and Matthew appear to have been derived straight from the Gospel of Mark, those later writers not even showing evidence of information other than what they got from Mark.

Mark explicitly names the four fishermen involved as being two sets of brothers: Peter and Andrew, James and John. Then Luke in turn comes to write his version of the event. He gives evidence that he is working directly from Mark's manuscript and thus knows good and well that Mark had named *four*. Nevertheless, he chooses to name only *three* fishermen. Luke's account does not name Andrew, shows no knowledge that Peter had a brother, and gives no hint that a fourth fisherman was even involved.

So what does Luke's freewheeling treatment tell us about his own literary methods and particularly about his opinion of the historical reliability of Mark's work? Is Luke suggesting that he finds Mark's account to be not simply outside the inspiration of the Holy Spirit but actually quite unreliable—needing rewording, revision, and actual correction at point after point? (Luke will use hardly as much as a sentence from Mark without revising it to some degree.)

No, such an attitude cannot be Luke's. The fact that he is eager to copy almost the whole of Mark's Gospel into his own is proof enough of the authority and respect he accords Mark. Regarding the "gospel truth" of its content, Luke certainly honors Mark's Gospel as an "inspired writing." And of course, in light of their subsequent places in the canon, it is clear that the church has always considered *both* Mark's and Luke's Gospels to be "inspired writings"—even if that necessarily shows one inspired writer being very free to change the wording, details, and even historical references in the inspired writing of the other. How can this be?

To me, the obvious answer is that "divine inspiration" was never understood as extending to matters of theologically inconsequential detail. Certainly Luke would be the first to deny that he was in any way challenging that Mark's Gospel was "the word of God." No, he accepts the authority of Mark on every matter of significance—even while feeling free to change details (whether it was three fishermen or four on the sea-shore). Luke exercises this freedom simply to make his own account serve *his* particular understanding and interests, to make a point perhaps just a bit different from the one Mark had been wanting to make. To put it otherwise, Luke's practice suggests that he saw the Holy Spirit as indeed interested in guaranteeing "the truth of the gospel"—but that the truth of the gospel was never intended to be synonymous with "the preservation of the historical exactitude of every jot and tittle of every writer's account."

And I propose that, if both Luke and the Holy Spirit have shown themselves ready to sit loose regarding all these minor Gospel discrepancies, perhaps we don't have to get uptight about them, either. They certainly do not indicate the infallible God's *absence* during the Scripture-writing process; they indicate only the fallible human-beings' *presence*.

Yet notice, now, the *positive* possibility provided by discrepancy of this sort. We have seen that Luke's decision to write "Andrew" out of the scene had to be deliberate rather than accidental. We can assume, therefore, that Luke must have had some *reason* for what he did; it can hardly be that he was simply playing fast and loose with the details Mark provided. So, if we can figure out *why* Luke felt led to make the change, that just might tell us something quite important about Luke's understanding of things. And it now gives me great joy to announce that Luke has been figured out. All you have to do is keep reading (for some number of pages) and you too will know. (Sorry about that, but you are not yet in a position to receive the truth. We have miles to go before we sleep.)

The Method

We are still committed to learn as much as Scripture can tell us about the Beloved Disciple, author of the Fourth Gospel. Yet in order to do that we must first discover the import of the fact that the Synoptic Gospels (Mark, Matthew, and Luke) focus on the Galilean Twelve whereas the Fourth Gospel focuses upon its Beloved Disciple.

Our method will be to do a great deal of comparing of the Gospels back and forth. Yet what we are after is not the customary "harmonizations" or what seems "the most historically plausible account." Most often in doing Gospel comparisons, we look for ways of explaining away apparent disagreements so that the different evangelists can be understood as actually telling a single story. Or we take their discrepant accounts and try to reconstruct the version that is the most historically plausible. Such an exercise is, of course, entirely proper and even necessary—yet this is not at all what we are undertaking now.

Our method will be what is technically known as "redaction criticism"—namely, the effort to read the mind of the final writer of each Gospel, to determine what he wanted to communicate in arranging his material and in wording it as he did. We are looking particularly for the "divergencies" between one Gospel and another. Once we find them, we will insist on letting them stand *as divergencies*—even where there might be perfectly obvious ways of harmonizing them. Thus we will regularly ask, Why would this writer have wanted *his* account, in this detail or that, to be different from the others? We will truly be "reading clues" in the manner of Sherlock Holmes.

We start from the premise that is now common to New Testament scholarship—namely, that the Gospel of Mark was the first to be written, and that, in writing their Gospels, Matthew and Luke each had a manuscript of Mark at hand and regularly copied from it. The Fourth Gospel, then, is a later work whose writer chose not to follow the common Markan "synopsis" that accounts for so much of the unity of the first three Gospels.

Explanation of the Chart

The chart here is a miniaturized version (done at great sacrifice of detail) of a large wall-hanging chart that made it possible to trace almost verse by verse the borrowing between the

"Borrowing" among the Synoptic Gospels

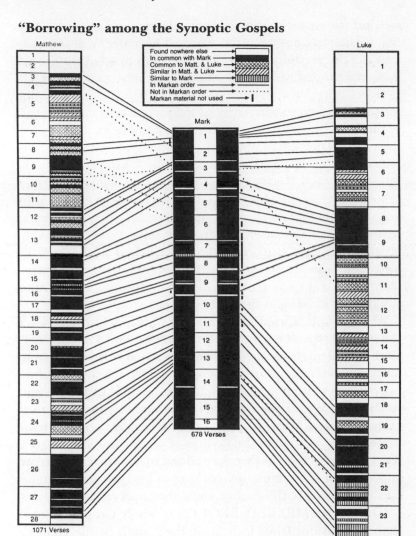

Gospels. Our specimen can present only in a general way the evidence that has led scholars to their conclusions regarding Gospel sources. Even so, it must be understood that the chart itself is not committed to any particular theory of *how* the Gospels came to be related as they are. It simply shows where we find the material that is identical—or very similar—from one Gospel to another (what we shall hereafter call "borrowings"). The chart does nothing more than present the factual data which must then be explained by this or that theory.

"Borrowing" would seem to be the only possible explanation for the close textual similarity of the material. If it were a case of the Holy Spirit's dictating the text to one Gospel writer and then to another, there obviously would be no variation or discrepancy at all. It would be inconceivable, for instance, that the Spirit would tell Mark to write that there were *four* fishermen called to be disciples and then tell Luke to write that there were only *three* (or that the Spirit would give Matthew a different version of the Lord's Prayer than he gave Luke). If, on the other hand, each Gospel writer had worked solely from his own memories, in complete independency from the others, then there is no way that the similarities among the Gospels could be as striking as they actually are.

A few scholars want to argue that Matthew is the original Gospel and that Mark is a *condensation* of it and Luke a *revised* edition. Throughout our treatment, however, we will assume the much more common theory—namely, that Mark, the short Gospel, was written first, and that Matthew and Luke are separately *expanded* versions of Mark. Presumably, in addition to using copies of Mark, both of these writers also had at hand copies of a collection of the sayings of Jesus (now identified as "Q"), which each in his own way added to his Markan borrowings while at the same time working in his own special materials. According to this theory, then, the chart reads as follows:

(1) The NUMBERED BLOCKS of each Gospel identify chapter divisions (thus indicating the length of the chapter, and finally of the book as a whole, on a scale of so many verses per inch). Thus we see that Luke has more *verses* even though Matthew has more *chapters*—and that Mark is but a bit more than half as long as either of the other two.

(2) In whatever column it appears, WHITE represents unique material in one Gospel that is quite unlike anything in

any other Gospel. For example, Mark has no "nativity stories" (and Q wouldn't even be expected to have had such). Accordingly, the "white" of Matthew's first two chapters shows that his nativity account is uniquely his own. Likewise, the "white" of Luke's first two chapters indicates not a commonality with the "white" of Matthew but the very opposite: Luke's nativity story is also uniquely his own. What we have here are two quite different accounts showing that neither Matthew nor Luke was familiar with the other's information.

Likewise, the scattered bars of white in the Mark column represent the very few verses not borrowed by either Matthew or Luke. The small patches of black that appear in a kind of dot-dash pattern close along on either side of the Mark column indicate that Matthew chose to reproduce almost the whole of Mark in his own Gospel—but that, for reasons of his own, Luke chose not to use considerable portions of Mark's chapters 6–9.

(3) Wherever it appears, SOLID BLACK represents material that Matthew and/or Luke have in *common* with Mark—material that Matthew and/or Luke likely borrowed from Mark. Of closely related significance, the VERTICAL HATCH represents material in Luke and/or Matthew *similar* to that in Mark, though not close enough to be called *common*. In most cases it probably represents Markan material that was *revised* in the borrowing process. However, it could identify cases in which Matthew and/or Luke took from sources of their own a story similar to (but not identical with) one from Mark and so passed over Mark's story in favor of their own particular version.

(4) The DOUBLE CROSSHATCH represents material *common* to Matthew and Luke (though obviously not taken from Mark, since none of it appears there). We are as much as forced to conclude that Matthew and Luke must have possessed—in addition to their respective copies of Mark—copies of another common document from which each borrowed. When tracked down in the Gospels, the material indicated by

the double crosshatch invariably is found to consist of "teachings of Jesus." Consequently, there is nothing to suggest that the Q document ever was a "Gospel" in the sense of being a *narrative* account of Jesus' life. Q has been preserved only in these borrowings of Matthew and Luke, although there may be a reference to it in Eusebius's fourth-century statement: "Matthew compiled 'the sayings' in the Aramaic language and each person interpreted them as he was able."

The SINGLE CROSSHATCH is a variation of the double crosshatch representing material in Matthew and Luke that is *similar* (though not close enough to be called *common*). For the most part, it is probably Q material that one or both of the writers revised enough to blur the obvious commonality.

Now, with both this chart and one of the Gospels before us, the procedure of the writer can become quite apparent. For instance, Matthew wants to begin his Gospel with narratives of Jesus' birth. Because neither Mark nor Q have anything to offer, his first two chapters must be drawn entirely from his own special sources. With chapters 3–4, then, he picks up on Mark's account, mixing in but little information from anywhere else. Chapters 5–7 are, of course, the Sermon on the Mount. Again, Mark (which is almost entirely narrative with comparatively little in the way of teaching material) is of no help, so Matthew constructs the Sermon by arranging and editing Q material. This material that Matthew presents as a three-chapter continuity is the same material that Luke scatters throughout the entire middle part of his Gospel. Finally, for his Passion account of chapters 26–27, Matthew copies directly from Mark—and then closes the whole with his own unique "white" account of Jesus' post-resurrection "last words."

The Fourth Gospel does not appear on our chart because there is nothing to qualify it for such appearance. Although it of course has a number of the same stories of Jesus that the Synoptics do, there is no evidence indicative of "borrowing," of common sources, of familiarity with anyone else's work, or of direct interconnections of any sort. The Fourth Gospel is truly an independent creation.

JESUS' DISCIPLES: A COMPARATIVE ANALYSIS

The Gospel according to Mark

We now begin our study proper by analyzing Mark's Gospel to discover just how he treats the Galilean Twelve and the individual disciples who make up that group. The Pauline letters and Acts make it clear that the young man John Mark was a personal acquaintance of the Apostle Peter and might well have gotten most of his information directly from him. Also, Mark wrote his Gospel as much as twenty years ahead of the other Gospel writers.

At ten different points in his Gospel, Mark refers to the disciple group as "the twelve." Matthew and Luke duplicate almost all the scenes in which these references occur. There are a few exceptions: neither Matthew nor Luke recounts Jesus' return to Bethany following the triumphal entry (whereas Mark records the event and mentions "the twelve"), and Luke's account of the Last Supper does not have Jesus identify his betrayer by dipping a sop. Mark, Matthew, and the Fourth Gospel all record the incident, but Mark is the only writer who identifies the betrayer as "one of the twelve."

In eight instances, then, Mark, Matthew, and Luke have the scenes in close parallel. In five of these instances, both Matthew and Luke follow Mark in speaking of "the twelve," yet in the three other instances, one or both of them choose the more general wording of "disciples" or "apostles" over the specific "the twelve." Clearly, neither Matthew nor Luke is as happy with the term "the twelve" as Mark is.

We now move from the Twelve as a group to a consideration of the constituent individuals.

1. Simon Peter

Peter is clearly the head (and perhaps something of a symbol) of the Twelve. But Mark's personal friendship with him may be another reason why Mark concentrates on Peter, casting him in fifteen different scenes. Both Matthew and Luke dupli-

cate almost all these—the exceptions being that Matthew omits
the scene of Simon and those with him seeking out Jesus in "a
lonely place," and Luke omits the scene about the barren fig
tree. The Fourth Gospel, on the other hand, has only one of
the same "Peter scenes" that Mark does (and greatly modifies
the role of Peter within it).

Mark's fifteen Peter scenes are as follows (Matthew and
Luke duplicate these unless otherwise noted):

(i) 1:16-20: Peter (with three others) is called from fishing on
the Sea of Galilee to become a disciple. Luke drops Andrew
from the group. The Fourth Gospel has no similar scene, but
presents Andrew as a disciple of John the Baptist who converts
to Jesus and then recruits his brother Peter.

(ii) 1:29-31: Jesus heals Peter's mother-in-law; Peter, Andrew, James, and John are present. Both Matthew and Luke
drop any mention of Andrew, James, and John.

(iii) 1:36: Simon and those with him seek out Jesus in a
lonely place. Luke drops the reference to Simon, and Matthew
doesn't use the incident at all.

(iv) 3:13-19: The Twelve are appointed and listed by name,
with Peter at the head. There are only minor variations of the
listing in Matthew and Luke; the Fourth Gospel has no comparable scene and never attempts anything like a list.

(v) 5:21-24: Jesus heals Jairus's daughter; Peter, James, and
John are present. Luke follows Mark in his recounting, but
Matthew drops the names of all three disciples.

(vi) 8:27-33: Peter makes his great confession. The scene
names no other disciples.

(vii) 9:2-13: At the Mount of Transfiguration, Peter is
prominent, but James and John are also present.

(viii) 10:28-31: "We have left everything. . . ." All three Synoptics attribute the statement to Peter.

(ix) 11:20-26: Peter sees the withered fig tree. Only Mark
names Peter. Matthew relates the incident without naming
Peter, and Luke doesn't even pick up the incident.

(x) 13:3-37: For the conversation regarding the signs of the end, Mark has present not only Peter but also James, John, and Andrew. Both Matthew and Luke record the scene but do not name any disciples at all, not even Peter.

(xi) 14:12-25: Interestingly enough, neither Mark's account of the Last Supper nor the accounts in the other Synoptics name any of the disciples (although Matthew editorially inserts the name "Judas" at one point).

(xii) 14:26-31: Peter vows that he will not deny Jesus. All three Synoptics name Peter here.

(xiii) 14:32-42: At Gethsemane, Mark names Peter, James, and John as present. For some reason, Matthew changes the reading to "the two sons of Zebedee" rather than naming James and John. And Luke writes the scene without naming any disciples at all.

(xiv) 14:53-72: Peter is in the courtyard of the high priest. Mark has Peter play this scene solo, and both Matthew and Luke follow suit. The Fourth Gospel has Peter accompanying "another disciple." In the courtyard, Peter denies Jesus. All *four* of the Gospels name Peter as the denier.

(xv) 16:1-8: The young man (angel) at the tomb instructs the women to "go, tell his disciples *and Peter*." Only Mark has this special naming of Peter. Matthew has only "go . . . tell his disciples." Luke doesn't even have the instruction, but has the women, on their own, telling "the eleven." And the Fourth Gospel is the only one having Peter (or any male disciples) actually at the tomb.

2. James the Son of Zebedee

Mark places James in a total of eight scenes. However, in six of these he does nothing but tag along with Peter. And less frequently is he even a tag-along figure in Matthew and Luke. In the appointing and listing of the Twelve, of course, James is mentioned in all the Synoptics. But both Matthew and Luke drop Mark's reference to James and John in their recounting of Jesus' healing of Peter's mother-in-law and in their account of the conversation about the signs of the end. Matthew drops

Mark's reference to James and John in his story of the healing of Jairus's daughter. And Luke drops Mark's reference to the two in his retelling of the Gethsemane event. Clearly, neither Matthew nor Luke is nearly as committed to the "Peter, James, and John" trio as Mark is.

In the remaining two scenes in which Mark mentions James (with John), James does do more than tag along with Peter:

(i) 1:19-20: Jesus calls James and John from being fishermen on the Sea of Galilee. Matthew follows Mark; Luke does too (but also inserts a quite different scene).

(ii) 10:35-45: In the dispute about greatness, Mark identifies "James and John, the sons of Zebedee," as the disputants. Matthew calls them "the sons of Zebedee" without naming them. Luke abbreviates the scene and does not name any particular disciples as being responsible for the dispute.

3. John the Son of Zebedee

With but one exception, Mark treats James and John in tandem—with Matthew and Luke also mentioning or dropping the brothers as a pair. Thus, the preceding analysis of James also holds precisely for John. The one exception is Mark 9:38-41: "We saw a man casting out demons." Mark has John speak these words, and Luke follows suit. Matthew doesn't even pick up the incident.

4. Andrew

Andrew is mentioned only in tandem with his brother Peter or along with Peter, James, and John. He is, of course, in the listing of the Twelve. In Mark's account, he along with his brother Peter is called from fishing to discipleship—though not in Luke's version of the same. Matthew drops Mark's reference to Andrew, as well as to James and John, in his version of the healing of Peter's mother-in-law. In their recounting of the conversation about the signs of the end, both Matthew and Luke drop all four names that Mark mentions—Peter, James, John, and Andrew.

5. *Philip*

6. *Bartholomew*

7. *Matthew*

8. *Thomas*

9. *James the Son of Alphaeus*

10. *Thaddaeus*

11. *Simon the Cananaean*

Apostles 5-11 Mark names only in his apostolic list and nowhere else. The one possible exception (a very problematic case) is whether the woman Mark identifies at the cross as "Mary the mother of James the younger and of Joses" (15:40) and at the tomb as "Mary the mother of Joses" (15:47) and "Mary the mother of James" (16:1) is to be thought of as the mother of James the son of Alphaeus.

12. *Judas Iscariot*

Judas Iscariot, of course, rates the attention he gets by being the betrayer. Yet, in Mark, that actually comes to very little.

(i) 3:13-19: In the apostolic list, of course, Judas is last, and even here he is identified as the betrayer. Both Matthew and Luke follow Mark in this.

(ii) 14:10-11: Judas goes to the chief priests to betray Jesus. Mark here calls him "one of the twelve," and both Matthew and Luke follow his lead.

(iii) 14:43-46: Judas leads the authorities to Jesus in Gethsemane. Mark again specifies him as "one of the twelve"—and again both Matthew and Luke follow suit.

Summary

Mark, in comparison with the other evangelists, shows a particular interest in specifying "the twelve" as a select and exclusive group of "disciples." Clearly, he sees Peter as the head—with James and John (and sometimes Andrew) ranking just below

Peter. However, he seldom uses these three in the action or tells us much about them. And apparently he has neither information about nor interest in the other eight.

Even when following Mark as their source, Matthew and Luke regularly rewrite his material in a way that plays down Mark's emphasis upon the Twelve as a group and his singling out of particular disciples by name.

The Gospel according to Matthew

We have seen that Matthew eliminates a number of the references to "the twelve" that he found in Mark. And apart from those he does retain, Matthew (even with all his new material) adds only one new occurrence of his own—an editorial note that, after Jesus commissioned the disciples, "these twelve [he] sent out" (10:5). Compared with Mark, Matthew clearly plays down the special status of the Twelve.

1. Simon Peter

Matthew reduces Mark's "Peter scenes" from fifteen to ten by omitting one scene and by writing Peter out of four others. Though almost half of Matthew's Gospel comes from sources other than Mark, the evangelist has but very little Peter material that is not Markan in origin—and probably all of that is from his own special sources rather than from Q. Apparently Mark was the only one of Matthew's sources that was much interested in Peter. Matthew gives us only two new Peter scenes, but he does add a reference to Peter in three other scenes:

(i) 14:28-31: In the midst of Mark's non-Peter scene of *Jesus* walking on the water, Matthew introduces the unique account of *Peter's* attempt to walk on the water.

(ii) 17:24-27: Matthew also introduces the unique account of Jesus' talk with Peter about paying the tax.

(iii) 16:17-18: This is not a new scene, but Matthew does add a unique statement in the midst of a Markan scene. Matthew (and only Matthew) has Jesus say, "Blessed are you, Simon

Bar-Jona! For flesh and blood has not revealed this to you, but my Father who is in heaven. And I tell you, you are Peter, and on this rock I will build my church," and so on. This, of course, is Scripture's most powerful affirmation of Peter's precedence; it is strange that Mark (the preeminent "Peter" Gospel) does not have it.

(iv) 15:14-15: The parable of the blind guides could be from Q, since Luke has it as well as Matthew. Yet only Matthew has Peter asking Jesus to explain.

(v) 18:21-22: Jesus' statement about forgiving seventy times seven could also come from Q; Luke has at least something of a parallel. But again, only Matthew has Peter asking how many times we should forgive.

The Rest of the Twelve

Matthew also differs from Mark in his treatment of the disciples other than Peter. Where Mark has Andrew in four scenes, Matthew writes him out of two of those—leaving him only in the apostolic list and in the scene in which he and his brother Peter are called to discipleship. Mark has James and John in eight scenes and John solo in one more. Matthew does not pick up the solo scene and writes James and John out of three more, reducing their role by half. Further, regarding these eleven, Matthew (out of his mass of non-Markan material) finds virtually nothing new. There are two exceptions:

(i) 10:3: In his version of Mark's apostolic list, Matthew adds the words "the tax collector" following the name "Matthew." Also, in 9:9, where he is following Mark's wording about "Levi the son of Alphaeus sitting at the tax office" (and regarding which Luke simply drops the words "son of Alphaeus"), Matthew changes it to read "*Matthew* sitting at the tax office." Every effort at correlation results in confusion, because the apostolic lists of all three Synoptics include both the names "Matthew" and "James the son of Alphaeus" but do not include the name "Levi" or designate anyone other than James as a "son of Alphaeus." Mark and Luke say that the tax collector was named "Levi" and do not so much as hint that he was one of the

Twelve; Matthew says that the tax collector was named "Matthew" and that he definitely *was* one of the Twelve.

(ii) 27:3-10: Here Matthew gives us a unique account of the death of Judas Iscariot that must come from his special sources. (Luke gives us a quite different account in the first chapter of Acts.)

Summary

Neither Matthew nor his non-Markan sources must have had any great interest in the Twelve. It is remarkable that so much tradition produces so little new information (i.e., so little more than Mark had provided) regarding them.

The Gospel according to Luke

As with the Gospel of Matthew, as much as half of Luke's material comes from non-Markan sources. We already have seen that Luke eliminated a number of Mark's references to the Twelve. And we now discover that, from the non-Markan half of his total material, he adds virtually no further references to them:

(i) 8:1-3: In a Markan passage about Jesus pursuing his ministry, Luke introduces a unique sentence: "And the twelve were with him, and also some women" (whom he proceeds to name).

(ii) 9:12: At one point in his account of the feeding of the five thousand, Mark has "disciples." Matthew follows that phrasing, but Luke changes it to "the twelve."

1. Simon Peter

Luke chose not to pick up one of Mark's fifteen "Peter scenes," and he wrote Peter out of three of the others. And now, out of his mass of non-Markan material, Luke comes up with just one new "Peter scene," which he uses to greatly modify one of Mark's:

Luke 5:1-11: Where Mark has Jesus simply calling Peter and

Andrew from their fishing, Luke has a unique and much more elaborate account. Jesus comes across two fishing boats on the seashore. He takes Simon's to use as a pulpit. Simon has just fished all night but caught nothing. Jesus sends him out again, and Simon makes a tremendous catch—which becomes Peter's conversion experience. "James and John, sons of Zebedee" are named as Peter's partners, but Luke fails to mention Andrew, Peter's own brother.

The obvious parallel between the "big catch" part of Luke's story and the "big catch" part of the Fourth Gospel's totally different story is striking.

Although the preceding is the only new "Peter scene" that Luke adds, he does show a minor tendency that likely is of only *editorial* rather than theological significance. Every once in a while he makes reference to Peter where his sources had not:

(i) 8:45: In the healing of the woman with a hemorrhage, Mark had "the disciples" make an observation; Luke has "Peter" make it.

(ii) 9:32: In using the Markan account of the Transfiguration (which, of course, was already a "Peter scene"), Luke simply inserts an additional, purely editorial naming of Peter.

(iii) 12:41: Presumably drawing on Q, Matthew and Luke recount the parable of a thief breaking into a house. Luke interjects a unique sentence: "Peter said, 'Lord, are you telling this parable for us or for all?'" Luke immediately returns to a recounting closely paralleling Matthew's, thus leaving Jesus to not so much as recognize the question—though my hunch is that Luke intends the implied answer to be "for all."

(iv) 22:8: When the disciples are preparing for the Last Supper, Luke inserts "Peter and John" where neither Mark nor Matthew names anyone.

(v) 22:61: Into Mark's obviously Petrine scene of Peter's denial, Luke makes this editorial insertion: "And the Lord turned and looked at Peter."

All these namings of Peter probably are to be seen as a literary "polishing of the text" rather than as signifying anything about Luke's view of Peter.

2. Andrew

Luke reduces references to Andrew to the absolute minimum: he names Andrew only in the apostolic list. Mark has him in four scenes. In failing to name him in his "call of the fishermen," Luke robs Andrew of one of those scenes and then writes him out of two others—apparently without finding anything more about Andrew in his non-Markan sources.

3. James & 4. John

Mark has James and John in eight scenes and John solo in a ninth. Luke writes them out of four of these scenes. One of the remaining scenes he replaces with his own unique version of "the calling of the fishermen," retaining James and John while dropping Andrew. But then, out of his own special material, Luke presents one new "James and John" scene—namely, the one in which the brothers want to call down fire on the unbelieving Samaritans (9:51-56).

Disciples Nos. 5-11

Regarding those whom Mark names only in his apostolic list, Luke finds nothing more to add. He does change the names that Mark and Matthew give to No. 10 and No. 11. It seems safe to assume that Luke's "Simon called the Zealot" is simply a variant for the Mark-Matthew "Simon the Cananaean." Simple elimination, then, would indicate that Luke's "Judas the son of James" must be the same person as the Mark-Matthew "Thaddaeus"—except that we do not know why Luke decided to make a change (perhaps to correct what he considered an error?). Interestingly enough, the Fourth Gospel (the one that doesn't even have an apostolic list) is the only one to agree with Luke that the Twelve included a "Judas" other than the one known as "Iscariot."

12. Judas Iscariot

Luke tells us little more about Judas than he got from Mark. Like Mark, he does not name Judas even in the Last Supper scene. Mark has no account of Judas's death. Matthew offers one. And Luke offers a quite different one—though in Acts rather than in his Gospel.

Summary

Like Matthew, Luke worked to cut back Mark's emphasis upon the Twelve, the role of Peter, and the second-level ranking of James, John, and sometimes Andrew. Even more striking is the fact that in his non-Markan sources Luke found even less new tradition about the disciples than Matthew did. It is clear that the Synoptic "disciple tradition" is attributable almost wholly to Mark and that Matthew and Luke were not particularly inclined to stress it.

We dearly wish we could know what was in the mind of Matthew and Luke at this point. Was it their assumption that Mark's sources (his data for writing) were not detailed enough to be precise about just who among the disciples was present or absent on any given occasion? And did they take this to mean, then, that singling out disciples was simply a matter of literary preference? Did Mark like the idea of populating his scenes with named disciples, while both Matthew and Luke preferred the simpler and more general method of naming no more characters than necessary? Or was it that Matthew and Luke, even if they did consider Mark's information accurate, did not feel themselves bound to preserve it at every point? Whatever the case, they obviously did not see Mark's authority as "an inspired writer" as extending to matters of inconsequential detail.

The Fourth Gospel (commonly known as John)

The most notable finding of this study will be how different the Fourth Gospel is from the Synoptics; we will discover but little actual connection or parallel between the two lines of tradition. So we can begin by noting that the Fourth Gospel's explicit acknowledgment of a special disciple-group known as "the twelve" is confined essentially to a single passage (6:66-71), which very passage also pointedly uses the term "disciples" to apply to more than just "the twelve":

After this many of his *disciples* drew back and no longer went about with him. Jesus said to *the twelve,* "Do you also wish to go away?" Simon Peter answered him, "Lord, to whom shall we go? You have the words of eternal life; and we have believed, and have come to know, that you are the Holy One of God." Jesus answered them, "Did I not choose you, *the twelve,* and one of you is a devil?" He spoke of Judas the son of Simon Iscariot, for he, one of *the twelve,* was to betray him. [Of course, wherever Scripture quotations include "the italics of emphasis," those are the work of no one other than Vernard Eller. All first-century writers could do was push harder with their pens.]

It can hardly be said that this is a recognition of any special virtue or authority in the Twelve, or even a compliment to them, for that matter—"and one of you is a devil."

The Fourth Gospel uses the term "the twelve" one other time—in 20:24. There, after introducing Thomas into the action (something the Synoptics never do), it identifies Thomas as "one of the twelve."

The Synoptics use the term "disciples" almost exclusively in reference to the Twelve. (Luke 6:17 is a problematic verse in which the evangelist may be referring to "a great crowd of his *disciples,*" and Matthew 28:19 does speak of making *disciples* of all nations.) But the Fourth Gospel uses the term quite differently—much more flexibly, openly, and inclusively:

(a) In most cases, the Fourth Gospel clearly does intend the special group—though, as we have seen, it is very shy about calling it "the twelve."

(b) However, there are any number of instances where that exclusive reference dare not be taken for granted. We need to guard against taking ideas from the Synoptics and simply assuming that they are those of the Fourth Gospel as well. We must leave the Beloved Disciple free to tell his story *his* way. And his way is to play down the Galilean Twelve.

He recounts the calling—or appointment—of only the following: (1) an unnamed disciple who is not necessarily one of
the Twelve, (2) Andrew, (3) Peter, (4) Philip, and (5) Nathanael, who is not necessarily one of the Twelve. In the course
of his book he further names and introduces into the action
(6) Thomas, (7) "Judas (not Iscariot)," and (8) Judas Iscariot.
Most significant, nowhere in the book does he so much as
name "James and John"; in a list in 21:2, he refers to "the sons
of Zebedee" as being present (though not as saying or doing
anything). Since he does not use the names "James and John"
in this reference, we can be certain the Beloved Disciple knows
the names of only six of the twelve disciples. And apart from
the fact that he names Peter as the leader and Judas as the
betrayer, he apportions individual prominence in a way entirely different from that of the Synoptic writers. Is it credible
that it could be Peter's first lieutenant, John the son of
Zebedee, who has given us a Fourth Gospel portrayal of the
Twelve that is so completely at odds with Peter's own picture—
assuming that that is what Mark's Gospel preserves for us?

(c) Finally, there are a number of references in which it is
clear that the Beloved Disciple is using "disciples" in a broad,
non-exclusive sense:

(i) 4:1: "Jesus was making and baptizing more *disciples* than
John [the Baptist]."

(ii) 6:60, 66: The first of the two verses says that many of
Jesus' *disciples* were having trouble with his teachings, and the
second says that many of these *disciples* "drew back."

(iii) 7:3: This reference will be of utmost importance regarding the Beloved Disciple himself. Jesus' brothers suggest
to him, "Leave here and go to Judea, that your *disciples* may see
the works you are doing." There is a strong implication that—
apart from the Galilean Twelve—there are disciples in *Jerusalem* who would like the Master to do more of his work among
them. The existence of a second, Jerusalem-based disciple
group will be fundamental to our understanding of the Fourth
Gospel—and here we are as much as told that such a group did
indeed exist.

In the next three instances Jesus (in his own teaching) speaks of "disciples" in a way that must go far beyond the Twelve. (With the exception of Matthew 28:19, the "Synoptic Jesus" never speaks so.)

(iv) 8:31: "If you continue in my word, you are truly my *disciples*."

(v) 13:35: "By this all men will know that you are my *disciples*."

(vi) 15:8: "Bear much fruit, and so prove to be my *disciples*."

(vii) 19:38: In this last example, the Beloved Disciple explicitly names as "a disciple of Jesus" Joseph of Arimathea, a Jerusalemite who obviously is not one of the Twelve—though Mark also identifies Joseph this way. Since the Beloved Disciple mentions Nicodemus in the following verse, he may intend that the same appellation apply to him also.

Summary: Obviously, the Beloved Disciple has no intention of denying the existence of the Galilean Twelve. He does, however, play down the centrality and exclusivity of that group and work at making "disciples of Jesus" more inclusive both in numbers and in geographical spread.

1. Simon Peter

The Fourth Gospel gives us nine different "Peter scenes." At first blush, this would appear not to compare too badly with the Synoptic high of Mark's fifteen scenes. However, closer examination shows that the Fourth Gospel treats Peter in an entirely different manner. For one thing, only one of the "Peter scenes" comes out of Jesus' *Galilean* ministry, the Fourth Gospel being very strongly oriented toward *Jerusalem*. What this means is that, in the Fourth Gospel, Peter does not get any of the big Synoptic scenes that establish his priority and significance as leader of the Twelve. The Fourth Gospel does not include the following: (1) either the Markan or the special Lukan version of Peter's being the first disciple called, (2) the healing of Peter's mother-in-law, (3) Peter's witnessing the raising of Jairus's daughter, (4) Peter's attempt at walking on the water, (5) Peter's great confession, (6) Peter's saying, "We have left everything to follow you," or (7) Peter's witnessing the Transfiguration.

In six of Peter's nine scenes in the Fourth Gospel, another, unnamed disciple (presumably the Beloved Disciple throughout) is present and manages to act in such a way as to outscore Peter. In addition, in none of his scenes does Peter come off looking particularly good. It cannot be said that the Fourth Gospel is out to put Peter down, though it is apparent that the effort is being made to establish the Beloved Disciple as having every bit as much claim to prominence as Peter.

(i) 1:35-44: This scene accompanies what would have been Jesus' baptism (if the Fourth Gospel had been specific about that) and thus is set near *Jerusalem.* Two of John the Baptist's followers—Andrew and an unnamed companion—convert to Jesus. Andrew then enlists his brother Peter. Here Jesus does name Peter in a way that clearly grants him headship. However, there is no denying that Andrew and his companion were made disciples before him and that Peter is actually a second-generation disciple. This picture, of course, is very different from the Galilean version of either the Mark-Matthew treatment or the special Luke treatment.

(ii) 6:66-71: This is the Fourth Gospel's one "Peter scene" out of Jesus' *Galilean* ministry. It is, of course, Peter who says, "Lord, to whom shall we go?" and proceeds to confess Jesus. Some harmonizers would make this scene a version of what the Synoptics present as Peter's "great confession," yet the text itself hardly supports that equivalence.

(iii) 13:1-30: This passage describes the Last Supper in the upper room. From here on, the setting, of course, is *Jerusalem.* The Fourth Gospel account—with the footwashing but no bread and cup—is quite different from those of the Synoptics, which speak of the bread and cup but not the footwashing. Matthew does give Judas Iscariot a line identifying him as the betrayer (clearly an insertion into the Markan account); otherwise, none of the Synoptics name any particular disciples or give them particular parts in the action.

However, the Fourth Gospel gives roles to Peter (an uncomplimentary one in the footwashing), Judas, and the Beloved Disciple. In what has to be a deliberate move, the Beloved Disciple is placed closer to Jesus (lying at his breast) in such a way that Peter has to use the Beloved Disciple as an intermediary in questioning Jesus about the betrayer. Some commentators argue that the Beloved Disciple *has* to be one of the Twelve, because only the Twelve were present in the upper room. Yet this is to take information from the Synoptics and impose it on the Fourth Gospel—where nothing is said that would limit the upper-room attendance one way or another.

(iv) 13:36-38: Jesus here foretells that Peter will deny him— clearly an uncomplimentary "Peter scene." The Fourth Gospel sets this incident in the upper room, although as part of Jesus' *discourse* rather than part of the *action sequence* preceding it. The Synoptics, on the other hand, place their parallel at the Mount of Olives, following the Last Supper.

(v) 18:1-11: This is the scene of Jesus' arrest in the garden. The Synoptic parallels name only Judas in this scene. All four Gospels agree that somebody cut off the ear of the high priest's servant. Yet only the Fourth tells us that the swordsman was Peter—another uncomplimentary "Peter scene."

(vi) 18:12-27: Here Peter denies Jesus in the high priest's courtyard. The Synoptics have Peter play this scene solo. The Fourth Gospel has another disciple there with him—and holding a conspicuous advantage: "Simon Peter followed Jesus, and so did another disciple. As this disciple was known to the high priest [presumably because he was an upper-class Jerusalemite], he entered the court of the high priest *along with Jesus,* while Peter stood outside at the door. So the other disciple, who was known to the high priest, went out and spoke to the maid who kept the door, and brought Peter in."

Once in, of course, Peter *denies* Jesus, although it is not so much as hinted that the other disciple did the same—a very

uncomplimentary "Peter scene." (And are not the Jerusalem
followers of the Beloved Disciple in effect here claiming that
"their boy," the other disciple, is the one eyewitness source
regarding the trial of Jesus?) Finally, in verse 26, we are subtly
reminded that Peter was indeed the ear-slasher.

(vii) 19:25-27: This can hardly be called a "Peter scene" in
that Peter isn't even present—yet that may be the very point of
the account. (The three Synoptics are in full agreement that no
representatives of the Galilean Twelve were present in any of
the action from Peter's denying of Jesus until, following the
episode at the tomb, the women simply reported to the Twelve
that Jesus was gone.) Yet, in the Fourth Gospel, present at the
cross are the Beloved Disciple and some women—presumably
from the Jerusalem group—but no Peter. Verse 35 pushes the
point of Peter's absence, the writer there specifying that "He
who saw it [the Beloved Disciple, obviously, and none of the
Galilean Twelve] has borne witness . . . , and he knows that he
tells the truth." None of the Synoptics is prepared even to hint
that the Galilean Twelve had representatives present (and
conversely, if the Beloved Disciple were actually John bar
Zebedee, the Synoptics would have been fully justified in making such a claim and would surely have taken the opportunity).

Moreover, in the scene, the dying Jesus names the Beloved
Disciple as son of his mother. Commentators agree that there
are theological overtones here going quite beyond the historical fact of what Jesus did regarding the care of his mother.
"The mother" is symbolic of "the church," and to be designated
as her "son" is to be recognized and blessed as "true Christian
offspring." Accordingly, this account says not necessarily that
the Galilean group is *outside* that blessing but that Jesus gave it
more pointedly and specifically to the Beloved Disciple and his
Jerusalem group. In any case, Peter isn't anywhere around for
this special endorsement.

(viii) 20:1-10: It is only the Fourth Gospel (with some minor
variant readings of Luke) that portrays Peter coming to the
tomb on Easter morning. (Did you know this before?) That

variant reading of Luke has Peter playing the scene solo. The Fourth Gospel plays it by the now-familiar pattern of competition. (The Fourth Gospel gives us some scenes referring to "another disciple" and some referring to "the disciple whom Jesus loved." This scene uses both terms together, as synonyms—an important clue that we are talking about one and the same person either way.)

Mary Magdalene discovers the empty tomb. "So she ran, and went to Simon Peter and the other disciple, the one whom Jesus loved [Galilee and Jerusalem are given parity], and said to them, 'They have taken the Lord out of the tomb, and we do not know where they have laid him.' Peter then came out with the other disciple, and they ran toward the tomb. They both ran, but the other disciple outran Peter and reached the tomb first." Peter is given the precedence of *entering* the tomb first, but the Beloved Disciple must be recognized as at least his equal as a witness of the Resurrection. (Question: Why would the Gospel of *Mark,* preserving the tradition of *Peter,* fail to place Peter at the tomb as a witness of the Resurrection, when the Fourth Gospel *does* have him there?)

(ix) 21:1-14: The risen Lord appears on the seashore. This chapter (a special appendix, as signaled by 20:30) is the most crucial of the Fourth Gospel's "Peter scenes" and is unique to this Gospel (though we have seen that Luke has what sounds very much like part of it in his special version of the calling the fishermen to be disciples). The Beloved Disciple is once more paired with (or against) Peter. This is the one instance in which the Beloved Disciple is found in Galilee rather than Jerusalem. Yet, clearly, it is also the very special case of this disciple (as an equal of Peter) having his own particular apostolate recognized by the risen Lord. I find this to be a truer way of reading this passage, rather than making any sort of effort to identify the Beloved Disciple with the Galilean Twelve.

Seven disciples are listed as present—though whether seven is meant as a significant number is impossible to say. Simon Peter properly heads the list as being the leader of the Twelve.

Next comes Thomas, whom the Synoptics know only as a name on their apostolic lists but who, in the Fourth Gospel, has just been given a prominent Resurrection role. Third is Nathanael; he is known (at least by this name) and given a role only in this Gospel—and we therefore cannot be certain that he is one of the Galilean Twelve. James and John are never named nor given roles in this Gospel, and the present mention of "the sons of Zebedee"—fourth and fifth on the list—is their one and only appearance. Plainly, the Fourth Gospel does not recognize them, along with Peter, as constituting the triumvirate that the Markan tradition presents. Numbers six and seven on this list are "two others of his disciples." The listing clearly is Fourth Gospel rather than Synoptic, so there is no reason to assume that the evangelist means to be confining it to the Twelve. The Beloved Disciple himself turns out to be in the group, and (because he regularly is anonymous) it is much more likely that he is meant to be included in the final "two others of his disciples" than to be identified as any one of the five who are named.

In the action of the scene itself, it is Peter who initiates and leads the fishing trip, but it is "that disciple whom Jesus loved" who first perceives the truth and thus, regarding the stranger on the seashore, cues Peter that "It is the Lord!" So, in this and other scenes without exception, it is the Beloved Disciple who has an edge on Peter rather than vice versa.

(x) 21:15-24: This is the conversation that takes place after Jesus appears on the seashore. Although the appearance and the conversation occur in unbroken sequence, verse 14 indicates that the two events are to be treated as separate scenes. The conversation between Jesus and Peter (vv. 15-19) gives complete honor to that disciple as the one whose denial has been forgiven, whose love for Jesus is full and sincere, and who now carries particular responsibility in "feeding my sheep."

But when, in verse 21, Peter turns to ask, "Lord, what about this man [the Beloved Disciple]?" Jesus responds, in effect, that nothing he has ever said to Peter or the Galilean Twelve gives that group any priority or status over the Beloved Disciple and his Jerusalem following: "If it is my will that he remain until I come, what is that to you?" This, surely, is the main thrust of the passage. Later, however, we will see that the rumor about the Beloved Disciple's not dying before the return of Jesus constitutes perhaps our very best clue as to who he is.

For present purposes, note particularly that it is from this dialogue that verse 24 immediately proceeds: "*This* is the disciple who is bearing witness to these things, and who has written these things; and we know that his testimony is true." The whole of the Fourth Gospel's authority and truth hangs upon the Beloved Disciple's having dominical credentials just as good as those of Peter himself. If the Gospel of Mark can claim Peter, the Fourth Gospel can just as truly claim the Beloved Disciple.

2. Andrew & 3. Philip

We recall that, in the Synoptics, Andrew gets no action of his own but is simply the tag-along brother of Peter. Mark notices him the most often, though only as the sometimes fourth after Peter, James, and John. Matthew drops Andrew from most of those scenes, and Luke compounds the injury by neglecting to mention him even in "the call of the fishermen"—leaving him only in the apostolic list.

In the Fourth Gospel, things are very different. It is James and John who get dropped. Andrew becomes a person in his own right (even named as the very first person to become a disciple of Jesus) and is regularly paired with Philip. He never is presented as a tag-along of brother Peter. Could it be that the Fourth Gospel stresses "Andrew and Philip" as a deliberate rebuttal to the Galilean tradition of "James and John"? Who can say? In any case, it is instructive to look at the Fourth Gospel references to Andrew and Philip.

(i) 1:35-51: We have seen that the Fourth Gospel account of Jesus' calling of his first disciples is totally different from that of the Synoptics. The locale is with John the Baptist near Jeru-

salem, rather than in Galilee. And the first people called are
not four Galilean fishermen but two of John the Baptist's disciples who convert to Jesus. One of these (we are told) is Andrew, the brother of Peter, who comes from Bethsaida on the
Sea of Galilee. We will argue that the other, who is unnamed, is
from the Jerusalem area. Thus, Galilee and Jerusalem are
given parity.

Andrew subsequently enlists his brother Peter—who, though
portrayed as anything but a tag-along, undeniably does come
into discipleship *after* Andrew and the other disciple are already there. Even so, Jesus clearly singles out Peter by naming
him "the Rock."

In this account, Jesus then goes to Galilee and calls Philip
(who in the Synoptics is only a name on the apostolic list), who
recruits Nathanael (who, at least by that name, isn't even
known to the Synoptic writers). It would seem that the Fourth
Gospel is out to challenge the Synoptic "pecking order"—giving Jerusalem parity with Galilee, making Andrew a disciple
in his own right, and perhaps even proposing "Andrew and
Philip" in place of "James and John."

(ii) 6:1-14: The feeding of the five thousand is one of the few
Galilean scenes that the Fourth Gospel shares with the Synoptics. In this scene, none of the Synoptics name any particular
disciples. The Fourth Gospel, however, gives speaking roles to
Andrew and Philip (and not to any "Peter" or to any "James
and John" with him).

(iii) 12:20-22: In a unique Fourth Gospel discourse scene
that is most crucially placed in the Passion sequence (just following the raising of Lazarus, Mary's anointing of Jesus, and
the triumphal entry, and just before the Last Supper), it is
Philip and Andrew who arrange for the "Greeks" to see Jesus.
Both "Philip" and "Andrew" are, of course, Greek names. It
could be that the Beloved Disciple wants to argue that his
Jerusalem tradition has been more open to outsiders than the
tradition of the Galilean Twelve has been. But again, it is dis-
tinctly not Peter, James, and John who take the lead.

(iv) 14:8-11 & 22: In its unique upper-room discourse, the

Fourth Gospel gives lines first to Thomas, then immediately to
Philip (no Andrew with him this time), and later to Judas (not
"Iscariot")—all three being disciples who, in the Synoptics, ap-
pear only on the apostolic lists.

(v) 21:1-2: It should be noted that Andrew and Philip do
not—either as a pair or as individuals—make the list of those
who met the risen Lord on the seashore. This might signify
nothing more than that the Writer knew they had not actually
been there. (Or it could be that the "two others of his disciples"
are Andrew and the Beloved Disciple—the very first "disciple
pair," here together again with Jesus at the very end.)

4. Thomas the Twin

The Synoptics know this disciple only as a name on the apostolic list and do not tell us that he was called "the Twin." The
Fourth Gospel, however, always identifies him as "the Twin"—
and puts him in four scenes, at least one of which is very
significant:

(i) 11:16: Upon hearing of the death of Lazarus and of Jesus'
decision to go to Jerusalem, it is Thomas who in effect says to
the other disciples, "Let's go with him—even if it means our
deaths."

(ii) 14:5: In the upper-room discourse (referred to in the
preceding section), Thomas speaks to Jesus just before Philip
does.

(iii) 20:24-29: In a major scene unique to this Gospel, it is
Thomas who expresses doubt regarding the resurrection of
Jesus and who thus becomes the most directly involved eyewitness of Christ's personal disclosure of proof of that resurrection. Before the addition of the Chapter 21 appendix, *Thomas's*
confession of faith—not Peter's nor the Beloved Disciple's—
stood as the climax and consummation of the Gospel.

(iv) 21:1-2: Finally, in the list of the seven disciples on the
seashore, *Thomas* is included as one of the three "special
Fourth Gospel disciples": Thomas, Nathanael, and the Beloved Disciple.

5. Nathanael

In John 1:43-51, Philip brings Nathanael to Jesus—who proceeds to honor him as "an Israelite indeed, in whom is no guile" who will see "heaven opened, and the angels of God ascending and descending upon the Son of man." And in his turn, it is Nathanael's privilege to make the first apostolic confession of faith (way ahead of Peter in the Synoptics). Otherwise, Nathanael reappears only in the final chapter, listed among the witnesses on the seashore. (This treatment—mentioning him in the last chapter after featuring him in the first—may or may not be a deliberate closing of the circle.) Nathanael may not get much of a notice, but it is a whole lot more than the Synoptics give their Bartholomew—and there is no real evidence that he is the same person as Nathanael.

6. Judas (not Iscariot)

All the Fourth Gospel gives this man is the speaking of one line during Jesus' Last Supper discourse (14:22). Yet in the Synoptics he didn't get even that much, and even his name was on only *one* of the three apostolic lists (Luke's).

7. Judas Iscariot

As is the case with the Synoptics, the Fourth Gospel knows Judas Iscariot almost exclusively as the betrayer. The difference between the Synoptic and the Fourth Gospel treatment of him may not be of particular significance.

(i) 6:66-71: It is in this passage—the one place where the Fourth Gospel has Jesus speak specifically of "the twelve"—that Jesus also says, "and one of you is a devil." The account then proceeds to name Judas as that one. Thus, the Fourth Gospel introduces the matter of Jesus' betrayal into the story very much earlier than do the Synoptics—and in direct connection with talk of "the twelve." (Is the Beloved Disciple taking a deliberate whack at the Synoptic tendency to exalt the Twelve?)

(ii) 12:4: All *four* Gospels have accounts—although with some puzzling variations—of a woman anointing Jesus with precious ointment. Three of these accounts (Luke excepted) have the disciples complain about the waste involved. The account in the Fourth Gospel is the only one identifying the complainer as Judas.

(iii) 13:21-30: Interestingly enough, the Synoptics recount the Last Supper without naming Judas (or any other particular disciples). When Jesus speaks of a betrayer, the disciples in general simply respond, "Is it I?" The exception in this regard is the Book of Matthew. Matthew editorially revised the Markan account to have Judas, specifically, say, "Is it I?" and Jesus respond, "You have said so." Conversely, the Beloved Disciple uses his Last Supper account to *emphasize* Judas's evil involvement. (Could it be that the Synoptists consistently want to soft-pedal Judas's Galilean Twelve connection, while the Beloved Disciple consistently wants to do the opposite?)

(iv) 18:1-11: The role that the Fourth Gospel gives Judas with regard to Jesus' arrest in the garden is not perceptibly different from that given him in the Synoptics.

The following chart summarizes the differences between the Synoptics and the Fourth Gospel.

The Synoptics	The Fourth Gospel
(1) These three Gospels agree with each other but not with the Fourth Gospel (until the Passion account).	(1) The Fourth Gospel uses quite different material and orders events quite differently (until the Passion account).
(2) Jesus speaks in brief, pointed sayings and parables.	(2) Jesus speaks in long, well-ordered discourses.
(3) Jesus is quite reluctant to talk about himself.	(3) Jesus talks mostly about himself.
(4) Jesus pursues his career (as brief as one year) mostly in Galilee, with only a final visit to Jerusalem.	(4) Jesus is frequently in Jerusalem (and his career lasts at least three years).

(5) The Synoptics evince a historical eschatology with a strong futurist orientation.

(6) Salvation is focused upon the faith community's continuous role in history.

(7) Salvation is portrayed as linear, historical progress toward the kingdom of God.

(8) The Synoptics were written earlier, A.D. 65ff.

(9) The Synoptics share a frame of reference with the Pauline epistles, Revelation, and most of the NT.

(10) The major view of the Synoptics grows out of mainline Judaism.

(5) The Fourth Gospel has a weak futurist orientation— i.e., "realized eschatology."

(6) Salvation is focused on the "whatever point in time" experience of faith in Jesus.

(7) Salvation is portrayed as divine communication between God and man.

(8) The Fourth Gospel was written later, toward A.D. 100.

(9) The viewpoint of the Fourth Gospel is unique to the Johannine literature.

(10) The Fourth Gospel expresses a minor view growing out of heterodox, intellectualistic Judaism.

THE GALILEAN TWELVE OF THE SYNOPTICS AND THE BELOVED DISCIPLE OF THE FOURTH GOSPEL

Our detailed analysis of the four Gospels has rather clearly exposed a *difference*—a "tension" if not an actual "conflict"— between the Markan-based tradition of a Peter-centered Galilean Twelve on the one hand, and the Fourth Gospel tradition of a Jerusalem-based Beloved Disciple on the other.

It must be said that the tension is all one-sided in that the Synoptics don't even recognize the existence of the other tradition. And that would seem to be the very heart of the problem for the Fourth Gospel. It gives no evidence of wanting to refute or deny the historical actuality of the Galilean Twelve but simply shows a desire to win recognition for its own tradition alongside that one. The basic argument seems to be that its tradition, compared with that of the Synoptics, has credentials that are equally as good, just as strong a connection to the historical Jesus, and just as much right to be considered dominical. There does not have to be any fight for superiority but simply a recognition of equality—which, finally, seems to be granted by the acceptance of both the Synoptics and the Fourth Gospel as part of the canon.

The preceding chart shows that there are radical differences of form and character between the Synoptics and the Fourth Gospel that raise knotty problems concerning the history of the man Jesus. Yet, at the time the Fourth Gospel was written, the central issue probably was not the historical one but the *theological* one of *how* Jesus was to be described, his person and work explained. And here the Synoptics and the Fourth Gospel betray very different theological worldviews.

The Historical Eschatology of the Synoptics

The frame of reference consistently assumed by the Synoptics is what we shall call historical eschatology. With that term we have in mind the assumption that "salvation," "the purpose of God," "the work of Christ," "the meaning of life"—all aspects of the faith—are meant to be understood in terms of God's directing human history toward the outcome he has in mind for it (call it "the new creation," "the kingdom of God," "the messianic age," "the day of the Lord," or what you will).

Consider, then, that this eschatological orientation inevitably makes theology not a matter of intellectual concept and abstract thought but a matter of historical narrative—dealing, thus, with the concrete particulars of social, public history. The goal of such theology is not developing systematic, rational theory but rather getting the story rightly told and interpreted. Accordingly, this tradition is best served not so much by profound "thinkers" as by reliable "witnesses."

In background, the historical eschatology of the Synoptics

undoubtedly took its rise from the mainline Old Testament development—notably, the histories (beginning perhaps with the promise to Abraham that "By you all the families of the earth shall [finally] bless themselves"), the greater number of Psalms, and the whole of the prophetic tradition. It would seem that modern scholarship has demonstrated conclusively that Jesus of Nazareth understood himself and his career primarily in terms of historical eschatology. The apostolic church then carried the idea forward directly from Jesus—to where Paul picked it up and developed it. The Gospel of Mark in particular, but the other Synoptic traditions as well, proceeded to make it *the* Gospel thematic. The Fourth Gospel and the three Epistles of John constitute perhaps the only New Testament literature betraying any different frame of reference. Historical eschatology safely can be called "the mainline tradition of Scripture."

And not only is it the case *that* the earliest Christian understanding was eschatological, but contemporary scholarship is now in almost full agreement as to *what* specific events (with what interpretations) made up the eschatological sequence of that earliest understanding. The chart on the following page represents my own version of what scholars now find the New Testament to be saying. (Of course, many of the *components* of this series do appear in the Fourth Gospel. Yet the point is that here the *interpretations* are different. In the Fourth Gospel, no individual component is itself "forward looking," is seen as part of an ongoing historical sequence, or, above all, is seen to be explicitly pointed toward the final outcome described in part six of the following chart.)

The Divine Communication of the Fourth Gospel

While historical eschatology asks the question, "Where is human history headed?" divine communication asks, "How can God, from the heavenly sphere, communicate his divine beati-

The Story of Jesus, Covenant Lord of the Coming Kingdom

1.
Earthly Ministry

Jesus' ministry has four principal components: (a) *proclamation* of the kingdom's coming, (b) *demonstration* of its powers, (c) *anticipation* of its future reality, and (d) *exhortation* to kingdom living.

2.
Passion & Death

In Jesus' passion and death are effected (a) the cutting (initializing) of the New Covenant in Jesus' blood, (b) the atonement accomplishing eschatological forgiveness of sin, and (c) God's final victory over the powers.

3.
Resurrection

Jesus' resurrection into the new life of the kingdom brings in its train both (a) the baptismal resurrection of believers and (b) the general resurrection at the end of the age.

4.
Exaltation

Jesus is enthroned as living Lord—the one made responsible for the remainder of the sequence—established at the right hand of power (graphically represented in his ascension).

5.
The Living Lord
in His Body
(as Holy Spirit)

Jesus' followers receive Pentecostal empowerment for (a) the evangelistic mission of eschatological "harvest" and for (b) newness of life—as individuals, but especially as communities of the end time.

6.
The Coming
of Jesus and/or
the Kingdom

Then comes "the end, when Jesus delivers the kingdom to God the Father after destroying every rule and every authority and power . . . that God may be everything to everyone."

—see 1 Cor. 15:20-28

tude (the Beloved Disciple regularly calls it 'eternal life') to human individuals in the sphere of the earthly, finite, and sinful?" Out of all the contrasts that could be developed between these worldviews, we will look at just two.

(1) Because it is *world-historical* in orientation, the eschatological tradition must also understand salvation in terms of *social* community. Of course, the individual does find *personal* salvation—but finds it precisely through becoming enlisted in the larger process of God's saving his creation. On the other hand, because divine communication is oriented primarily toward a believer's finding "eternal life," it inevitably sees salvation in the more individualistic terms of a person's coming to faith in Jesus.

(2) Because it wants and needs only *witnesses* who can get the *narrative* of God's story rightly told and interpreted, the theology of historical eschatology is essentially simple and available to anyone without particular intellectual qualification. A fisherman like Peter will make just as good an apostle as a rabbinical egghead like Paul. Quite different is the language of divine communication in the Fourth Gospel, which speaks much more to readers who can handle matters of intellectual comprehension, creative insight, abstract conceptualizing, and philosophic theory-building. It may well be true that the Fourth Gospel is written in the plainest and simplest Greek of them all—and that (on one level) it has a message available to the most common of readers. Yet it is also true that this Gospel has other levels of meaning much more subtle and sophisticated than anything found in the Synoptics. Throughout Christian history there has been a notable tendency for intellectuals to gravitate toward the Fourth Gospel as their favorite.

I have no interest in pitting these two modes of apprehension against each other, puffing one up and putting the other down. My only concern here is to show that these two New Testament traditions appeal to two different sets of mind. Yet what this suggests is that the Fourth Gospel comes out of a background different from that of biblical eschatology. Its predecessors seem rather to have been the Old Testament "wisdom tradition," the more speculative and theorizing wing of rabbinical Judaism, and apparently even influences from Hellenistic philosophy. Of course, this tradition does stand as reputable and well-grounded—yet it also has to be counted as minor and heterodox in comparison with the dominance of biblical eschatology.

Now if the Fourth Gospel was written out of a sense that it was wrong for the church to ignore and dismiss that intellectualist tradition by giving attention solely to the eschatological Synoptic one, then it has been just as wrong for the later church to reverse that evaluation. Up until quite recent times, biblical scholarship has shown its own strongly pro-intellectualist bias by favoring the Fourth Gospel. One way it has done so is by arguing that the two Gospel types are to be read in sequence, marking a *progress* in Christian thought. The intellectuality of the Fourth Gospel marks a theological sophistication that overcomes and supersedes the primitivism of historical eschatology; the Beloved Disciple's theology of religious experience (if that is what it is) gives us a way of escaping the unscientific crudity of supernaturalism and public miracle.

To my mind, one of the most damaging tendencies of Christian theology has been the inclination to assume that the more subtle, sophisticated, and intellectualized an explanation is, the *truer* it is. But of course, this doesn't begin to follow— particularly regarding *God's* truth, which we must assume he has revealed for the benefit of all. Yet I would guess the same bias is at work when we explain that the Fourth Gospel is the *spiritual* one—without even pausing to say what we mean by "spiritual." What can we mean except "having less to do with actual historical reality and more to do with ideas, abstractions, and generalizations"? And these we automatically take as being superior to nuts-and-bolts historical actuality.

Another way in which this intellectualist bias shows up is in an idea that dates at least as far back as John Calvin—namely, that the Fourth Gospel is our key to understanding the Synoptics. On the contrary, it strikes me that if one thing is clear it is this: using the Fourth Gospel as the key will guarantee a misunderstanding of the Synoptics. These two kinds of Gospel represent *different* mind-sets and *independent* voices. Each has to be understood on its *own* terms. Any attempt to merge them, to try to make them speak with a common voice, or to use one to unlock the other cannot work except to the detriment of both. So I'm with the Beloved Disciple himself in not claiming that his tradition stands superior to that of the Galilean Twelve or that his word should displace theirs; I, like him, am just complaining that theirs should not be taken as God's *only* word. Even though the Fourth Gospel is a minor voice, it deserves a hearing, too.

THE CREATION OF THE FOURTH GOSPEL

The Source and the Writer—Dividing the Labor

Does our analysis enable us to say anything about who the Beloved Disciple was or how his book came to be written?

I think it is safe to say that, although the Beloved Disciple is claimed as the *Source* of the book, that does not necessarily (nor even likely) mean that he is its actual *Writer*. The eyewitness testimony about the Crucifixion (19:35) reads, "*He* who saw it has borne witness—*his* testimony is true"—not "*I* saw it, and *my* testimony is true." The original, chapter-20 ending of the book says, "These are written . . ." rather than "I have written these. . . ." And the later, chapter-21 ending says, "This is the disciple . . ." rather than "I am the disciple. . . ." And the remainder of that verse, though it reads that he is the one who "has written them," could as accurately be translated to say that he is the one who has "caused these things to be written."

If the *Writer* was a close colleague and follower of the *Source*, it is quite understandable that he would refer to his master by using the honorific title "the disciple whom Jesus loved." If, however, the Writer was the same person as the Source (was himself the Beloved Disciple), it is hard to believe that he would be so presumptuous as to write a document identifying *himself*, against all others, as "the disciple whom Jesus loved."

The epistles of 2 John and 3 John each open with the writer's identifying himself as "the Elder." And second-century church tradition tells us there was a man known as "John the Elder" who was associated with "John the Disciple, son of Zebedee" in the writing of the Gospel. We will need to do a great deal more testing before we decide whether to identify this "John-Z" as the Beloved Disciple. However, it does not seem too incautious a move to suggest that "the Elder" of 2 & 3 John is tradition's "John the Elder" and is the *Writer* of the Gospel, though not the Beloved Disciple who is its Source.

Our theory that there were two people, a Source and a Writer, certainly would still leave the Beloved Disciple (the Source) responsible for all the memories of Jesus included in the Gospel—and undoubtedly responsible for the basics of that Gospel's theology as well. The assumption must be that the Beloved Disciple was around long enough to guide the development both of his own community of disciples and of his whole school of thought. John the Writer, of course, would have to take responsibility for many of the details of form and interpretation we find in the Gospel, but we can take for granted that he did his very best to be as true to his Source as he could manage. The finished Gospel, then, *can* be taken as an accurate and faithful expression of the memories and mind of one of Jesus' disciples whom his followers had come to know as "the disciple whom Jesus loved."

John bar Zebedee—Unlikely Candidate

As we come to the problem of naming that Beloved Disciple, we will insist upon one rule—namely, if we are to find any clue to his identity, it will have to come from the Fourth Gospel itself. Since it is the only document that even knows of a Beloved Disciple, it is the only document that can be of any help in identifying him. To put the matter most pointedly, we dare not use data from the Synoptic tradition to draw conclusions about what must have been true for the tradition of the Fourth Gospel. Thus, simply the fact that the Markan tradition saw John the son of Zebedee (John-Z) as an at least somewhat prominent figure is no indication that Fourth Gospel tradition saw him the same way. Similarly, we must reject the reasoning noted earlier: that because the *Synoptics* imply that only the Galilean Twelve attended the Last Supper, and because the *Fourth Gospel* places the Beloved Disciple there, the Beloved Disciple must be one of the Twelve.

Thus, what we now need to see is that—if we confine ourselves to the Fourth Gospel's own evidence—there is no way anyone could ever have come to the conclusion that the Beloved Disciple was even one of the Galilean Twelve, let alone John-Z. This identification is based *solely* upon a late-second-century church tradition to that effect, a tradition that came to be supported with arguments from the *Synoptics*. As we have seen, if it were the Synoptics that called this beloved one "a disciple," that *would* have been as much as to identify him as one of the Galilean Twelve. But when it is only the Fourth Gospel that calls him "a disciple," nothing of the sort is implied.

Consequently, I am now ready to propose that the Fourth Gospel not only fails to even hint that its Beloved Disciple is John-Z but actually suggests that such is one of the poorest guesses that could be made. The fact that the *Writer* of the book was probably a man named "John," plus the easy assumption that, since the Beloved Disciple is called a "disciple," he must have been one of the Twelve—my hunch is that these considerations in themselves would have been enough to latch the tradition onto John-Z. But here follow our arguments to the contrary:

(1) When the Synoptics make it so clear that John-Z was a *subordinate* of Peter, is it credible that John-Z himself would

have been party to a rival Gospel in which he is portrayed as a
rival of Peter's? Hardly; that Beloved Disciple rival just has to
be someone other than John-Z.

(2) All we know of John-Z indicates that he was a Galilean
fisherman. This makes it very hard to find in him the intellectual and educational background requisite for the founder of
a theology as sophisticated and subtle as the Fourth Gospel's
divine communication. John-Z probably didn't even have the
vocabulary to do the intellectualist philosophizing that the Beloved Disciple does with, say, "the Word" *(Logos).*

(3) If John-Z was as completely part and parcel of the Galilean Twelve as the evidence indicates, it will be very difficult to
explain how he came to break entirely away from that community's memory of, understanding of, and theological interpretation of Jesus—to go off in a quite different direction.

(4) If the Beloved Disciple was John-Z, that means the ideo-
logical tension developed *within* the community of the Galilean
Twelve rather than *between* the Galilean Twelve and an outside
community. If such is the case, it is hard to see how the Synoptic tradition (which is, of course, that of the Galilean Twelve)
could have avoided any knowledge or hint of this split within
its own ranks. Could that tradition write its Gospels showing
John-Z to be simply "one of the boys" if it were common knowledge that he had broken away to found a new school of
thought and new communities on his own? If, on the other
hand, the Beloved Disciple were someone else who had never
been an integral part of the Galilean Twelve community, it is
easy to understand how the Synoptic tradition could have
chosen simply to ignore the existence of the small, alien, off-
shoot tradition that had never been part of the Synoptic story
anyhow. Indeed, it was probably this very ignoring that moved
the Beloved Disciple to argue his case in the first place.

NOTE: By the way, of the Synoptic traditions, it is uniquely
that strand of material known only to Luke that betrays any
awareness of distinctive Fourth Gospel memories. There are
perhaps seven points at which Luke's Gospel shows special

agreement with the Fourth Gospel: (i) Though he puts it in an entirely different setting, Luke does have a similar story about fishing all night, catching nothing, and then—at the instigation of Jesus—making a miraculous catch. (ii) It could be out of a knowledge of the Fourth Gospel's tradition of Andrew being the first-called disciple that Luke chose to leave Andrew out of his scene of the calling of the fishermen. (iii) Luke knows about the sisters Mary and Martha (who otherwise appear only in the Fourth Gospel)—but apparently not their brother Lazarus. (iv) Only Luke and the Fourth Gospel agree that one of the twelve disciples was a "Judas" other than the one called "Iscariot." (v) We later will explore the possibility that, among the Synoptists, only Luke knew what the Fourth Gospel explicitly states—that the woman who anointed Jesus was named "Mary." Further, (vi) only in Luke and the Fourth Gospel does this woman anoint Jesus' *feet* and then dry them with her *hair*. (vii) We have seen that it is only a minor variant reading of Luke that agrees with the Fourth Gospel in placing *Peter* at the garden tomb on Easter morning.

Of course, I do not mean to imply that the Fourth Gospel was already in writing at the time Luke wrote his Gospel and that Luke had seen it. Rather, Luke is the one evangelist who claims to have done deliberate research in preparation for his writing. Accordingly, he may have been the one willing to seek out and interview the Beloved Disciple (or some of his followers) and incorporate at least a bit of the Fourth Gospel version into his own account.

(5) If the Beloved Disciple is John-Z, then the rather clear Fourth Gospel pattern of "Galilee / Peter / rustic eschatology" balanced against "Jerusalem / Beloved Disciple / sophisticated theology" won't begin to work; John-Z is too decidedly of the wrong group.

(6) We need to be quite clear about in which respects the *Writer* of the Fourth Gospel is shy in speaking of the Beloved Disciple and in which respects he is not. He obviously is shy about *naming* the Beloved Disciple; he is not at all shy about

introducing him into the account. Quite the contrary, if (as seems very much the case) one of the goals of his writing is to establish the credibility and authority of that disciple, then I think it safe to assume that the Writer has recorded every significant appearance of the Beloved Disciple he honestly could. There would be no cause for him deliberately to suppress information helpful to his argument.

Thus, the only conceivable reason for his not giving us Beloved Disciple scenes out of the Galilean phase of Jesus' ministry is that the Beloved Disciple was not there. John-Z obviously *was* there; ergo, John-Z is not the Beloved Disciple. Or, to state the matter differently: If John-Z *is* the Beloved Disciple, then clearly the Beloved Disciple was present at Jesus' transfiguration. If the Beloved Disciple *had* been present, he undoubtedly would later have recounted that story to his community along with the other stories he told them. And if the Beloved Disciple had told this story, John the Writer would have been familiar with it. And if familiar with it, the Writer certainly would have wanted it in the Fourth Gospel as one of the very best stories for his purpose. So, if the Transfiguration could honestly have been presented as a Beloved Disciple scene, it would surely be in the Fourth Gospel. It is not there—which is proof enough that the Beloved Disciple was not present. John-Z *was* present—which is to say that he is *not* the Beloved Disciple. (Sherlock would have had no trouble following that—even if you did.)

(7) Similarly, of crucial importance to the Writer's purpose would be a scene recounting how the Beloved Disciple became a disciple of Jesus in the first place—that proof of qualification perhaps taking precedence over whatever other scenes the Gospel might give him. Consequently, if (as per John 1:35-42) the second disciple of John the Baptist (who, along with Andrew, initially converts to Jesus) is the Beloved Disciple, then the Writer has the right scene put in the right terms and in just the right spot: Jesus' first-called disciples are the Beloved Disciple in tandem with a representative of what will become the

Galilean Twelve. However, if Andrew's companion is John-Z, the pattern doesn't hold. And unless that companion *is* the Beloved Disciple, the Fourth Gospel stands without any account of its hero ever being made a disciple—which, particularly in an argument as sophisticated as that of our Writer, would amount to an incredible oversight.

However, the evidence suggests anything but oversight. Occasionally the Fourth Gospel uses the phrase "the disciple whom Jesus loved"; more frequently it uses the wording "another disciple" or "the other disciple." Once (in 20:2) the text reads, "the other disciple, the one whom Jesus loved." Thus it seems safe to assume when the Writer makes any reference to another, unnamed disciple, he has in mind this one particular disciple whom Jesus loved. It is beyond credibility that the Writer has a number of different disciples that he is committed to keeping anonymous.

The account of Jesus' acquiring his first two disciples is just slightly different. Neither the phrase "the disciple whom Jesus loved" nor the phrase "the other disciple" is used. Rather, in 1:35-42, the matter reads thus: John the Baptist is standing with "two of his disciples" who, at Jesus' approach, hear their master speak in recommendation of him. "The two disciples heard him say this, and they followed Jesus." Then, upon concluding his account, the Writer notes, "One of the two who heard John speak, and followed him [Jesus], was Andrew, Simon Peter's brother." There is obviously a second disciple who converts along with Andrew—though no sort of individual reference to him is made.

Even so, I find more than enough circumstantial evidence to establish that this "played-down" disciple was indeed he who later came to be known as the one Jesus loved. Consider also what the Gospel itself makes certain—namely, that the Source (if not the Writer) of the Gospel is this same Beloved Disciple. And what I find in his Gospel is evidence aplenty that he had indeed once been a disciple of John the Baptist.

Notice, first, that in his great Prologue of 1:1-18 the author takes pains to insert the two careful footnotes of verses 6-8 and verse 15. In both notes he makes the same dual point: (a) that the Baptist was a true servant of God deserving the highest respect, but (b) that he himself was not the "Logos/Light" who became flesh—because that, of course, was *Jesus*. The passage immediately following (1:19-34) is, then, this Gospel's account of John the Baptist—the entire content of which is the Baptist's push-push-pushing the point that only Jesus is "the One" and John himself merely a witness and helper.

Now why, I ask, should the Beloved Disciple find this point so vitally important, while the Synoptic writers are content simply to mention it as obvious, without any felt need to argue it in detail or at length? The explanation (I propose) is that the man behind this Gospel (the Beloved Disciple, of course) had in fact been a disciple of John the Baptist and knew that this background of his was common knowledge. He had probably come under criticism—his Jewish enemies even accusing him of being a fence-jumper and traitor for the way in which he had deserted the Baptist in order to join Jesus.

In such case it would, of course, be important to set straight at the very outset the facts of the matter—namely, that no disloyalty had been involved, that it was the Baptist himself who was most insistent about his being merely a forerunner who was meant to *serve* Jesus rather than compete with him. Thus, the very treatment accorded the Baptist in this Gospel is evidence that the Beloved Disciple was indeed that unnamed follower who, along with Andrew, had converted to Jesus.

And if the case be as we have shown it, then the traditional idea that this Beloved Disciple was also none other than the fisherman disciple John-Z can't be made to fit the scenario at all. We already have noted that the Fourth Gospel never so much as names John-Z (a passing reference to "the sons of Zebedee" in its final chapter being the closest it comes to doing so). The Fourth Gospel provides us absolutely no information regarding John-Z; for that, we are dependent wholly upon the Synoptics. And those three Synoptics are unanimous in placing John-Z among the fishermen whom Jesus approaches on the seashore *in Galilee* to commandeer into his service as disciples. Surely the Synoptic wording more strongly *prohibits* rather than *suggests* the possibility that John-Z already was a disciple who had made his commitment somewhat earlier *down south*. Indeed, the Synoptic evidence points to the conclusion that John-Z became Jesus' disciple on the Galilean seashore and that, therefore, the follower of the Baptist who earlier, down south, had become Jesus' disciple, subsequently to be known as "the disciple whom Jesus loved"—he must have been someone else.

Of course, the same problem presents itself when the Fourth Gospel tells us that "Andrew, the brother of Peter" was another follower of the Baptist who, there in the south, converted to Jesus—while the Synoptics clearly claim Andrew as one of the commandeered Galilean fishermen. Yet with "Andrew" there are important differences. For one, the earlier case dealt with a Fourth-Gospel down-south convert who is completely *unnamed*. Tradition has *arbitrarily* (without any sort of textual support) identified him with a particular one of the four *named* Galilean fishermen. However, in the present case, "Andrew, the brother of Simon Peter" is named by name both in the down-south Fourth-Gospel account and in the Galilean Synoptic one. This is far from *arbitrary;* there is here no way of *denying* the connection.

The other difference is the more intriguing and compelling. Because it is clear that Luke used Mark's Gospel as one of the sources for writing his own, it is indisputable that he was well aware that, in the "calling of the fishermen" (1:16-20), Mark explicitly named the two sets of brothers—first "Simon and Andrew" and then "James and John." Yet, even though Luke had that knowledge, he managed to write his own version of the incident (5:1-11) without acknowledging anyone named "Andrew," without mentioning that Peter even had a brother, without recognizing that any more than *three* fishermen became disciples. In fact, in the entire Gospel of Luke, the apostolic listing of 6:12-16 is the one and only notice that there ever was an "Andrew" who was Peter's brother.

So, why this perversity on Luke's part? I see but one explanation: Luke (I propose) knew the truth (as apparently neither Mark nor Matthew did) of what the Beloved Disciple later wrote—namely, that Andrew was the very first of Jesus' disciples, who had become such by "transferring" from John the Baptist. This means that if Luke portrayed Andrew as becoming a disciple along with the other three fishermen, he would knowingly be giving an inaccurate account. Luke may have assumed that Andrew wasn't even present on the seashore—or that, even if Andrew was there, he ought not simply be lumped in with the other three "first timers." So apparently Luke decided that he didn't even want to recount the earlier story of Andrew (which was his literary privilege). And in light of that choice, I think I agree with Luke that the easiest way of keeping straight and unconfused the line of the story he really wanted to tell was simply to drop complicating "Andrew" entirely from the picture—it was either that or else distract the readers by having to tell the whole story of Andrew.

In any case, the reconciling of Andrew's Fourth Gospel "down south" discipleship with his Synoptic "up north" discipleship—this is a very much clearer, easier, and more certain move than the entirely unsupported speculation that Andrew's unnamed "down south" companion is the same person as his "up north" fishing neighbor, John-Z. Luke, at least, does not buy this idea; otherwise, logic would dictate that he treat the two men the same, dropping "John-Z" right along with "Andrew" so as to avoid suggesting that John-Z also first became a disciple on the seashore (which, of course, is not the case if he is indeed the Beloved Disciple).

No, I submit that neither the Fourth Gospel nor the Synoptics will "work" (they won't "mesh") unless, after the two followers of the Baptist convert to Jesus, Andrew goes north to be the point of contact in forming the Galilean Twelve and the Beloved Disciple stays south to be the point of contact for his own Jerusalem disciple-group (and John-Z is obviously no one who stayed south).

THE NAME OF THE BELOVED DISCIPLE

The preceding discussion was meant to establish the great unlikelihood that the Beloved Disciple could be John-Z. Yet perhaps even more significant is the fact that the Fourth Gospel itself contains not the slightest hint that John-Z is its man. If all we had was the Fourth Gospel, "John-Z" (whose name we wouldn't even know) would be nothing but a wild guess—with either "Andrew," "Philip," "Thomas," or even "Nathanael" having better chances of being right. However, if we take the approach that the Fourth Gospel *has* to provide its own answer, then there is only one person who comes close to qualifying as the Beloved Disciple. Either the Beloved Disciple is LAZARUS—or else we don't have a ghost of a clue as to who is.

If "Lazarus" is the given answer, the case is *subtle*—which is just what we'd expect from this Writer, whose presentation is subtle in all respects, theologically and otherwise. All the Gospel's mentioning of Lazarus (at least under the name "Lazarus") occurs from 11:1 through 12:19—and this will turn out also to be *the* pivotal passage of the Writer's finely constructed Gospel. Let's see just how much this passage can tell us.

Jesus is already in Judea, in the environs of Jerusalem—in fact, "across the Jordan [at] the place where John at first baptized" (10:40)—presumably the very spot where Lazarus (now) originally became Jesus' disciple . . . if he is indeed that other follower of John the Baptist who subsequently became Jesus' Beloved Disciple. And recall that, in that earlier scene (1:19, 24), the account has Jewish bigwigs hanging around—just as will be the case in this next one.

"Now a certain man was ill, Lazarus of Bethany" (11:1). And when his sisters decide to inform Jesus, the message they send is "Lord, he whom you love is ill" (v. 3). That subtle line, recall, is given us by the same subtle Writer who will from this point forward keep us subtly reminded of "the disciple whom Jesus loved." And it is only these two people (or one person), Lazarus and the Beloved Disciple, regarding whom the Writer ever uses this language. The only other recipient of comparable love-talk is Peter at the seashore—though there it is "Peter, do you love *me?*" not "Lazarus, you are the one *I* love!"

But if perchance you missed the significance of verse 3, the Writer will run it past you several more times. "Now Jesus loved Martha and her sister and Lazarus" (v. 5). In verse 11 Jesus says to the Galilean Twelve, "*Our friend* Lazarus has fallen asleep." (From the pen of the long-after-the-fact Writer, this could be a way of saying, "Hear this, you mainline apostolic eschatologists: Jesus identified this Jerusalemite egghead deviationist as 'our friend.'") "Jesus wept" (v. 35). "So the Jews said, 'See how he loved him!'" (v. 36). This last notice is of particular importance.

As we will proceed to discover, Lazarus performs a function in the Fourth Gospel for which the Synoptics simply have no equivalent—namely, he is the point of contact between Jesus and the Jewish dignitaries (official high-class Judaism). The Galilean Twelve of the Synoptic tradition just do not have the wherewithal for bringing the gospel to—or expressing it for— that intellectual community. And here in verse 36, intellectual Judaism confirms the fact that Jesus did indeed love his disciple Lazarus. Yes, the Writer has to do it subtly, but what else could he be saying except that Lazarus is indeed the disciple whom Jesus loved?

Now, based on the fact that, in the Fourth Gospel, Lazarus is the only named disciple of whom it is also said that Jesus loved him, we have set up the hypothesis that Lazarus is indeed the Beloved Disciple. So, assuming that identity, we will proceed to test the hypothesis by seeing how well Lazarus fits the role (the very move Sherlock would make at this point).

Lazarus and the Jewish Intelligentsia

If both Paul himself and his Writer (Luke in the book of Acts) saw him as "Apostle to the Gentiles," there is the same possibility that Lazarus, the Beloved Disciple, and his Writer (El-

der John) saw him as "Apostle to the Jewish Intelligentsia."
The Fourth Gospel (I propose) presents Nicodemus, Lazarus,
and Joseph of Arimathea as being pretty much of a kind. All
three are essentially Fourth Gospel figures; only one of them,
Joseph, is as much as mentioned in the Synoptics. They represent a type the Synoptics simply do not know—namely, trul·
devout yet open-minded Jewish leaders of the educateu,
cultured upper-class.

John 1:19-28 makes it clear that people of this sort were
interested in John the Baptist and were around when he
deferred to Jesus as the one who outranked him. And still very
early on, John 3 has Nicodemus—just such a Jewish leader—
seeking out Jesus. In this context, then (quite different from
the Synoptic one), it is not incredible that Lazarus could have
been a similar teacher who had become a convinced follower
of the Baptist and who later (along with Andrew) had followed
the Baptist's cue in switching to Jesus. The fact that the event
happened near Jerusalem (and thus Bethany), the fact that
Jewish leaders were on hand, the fact that Lazarus later appears as Jesus' old and dear friend—everything fits.

In this regard, notice another point at which Lazarus makes
a much better candidate for author of the Fourth Gospel than
does John-Z. In the Fourth Gospel (yet only in the Fourth
Gospel) there is the story of the Jewish head rabbi Nicodemus
(Jesus calls him "*the* teacher of Israel"): how he initiated an
interview by coming to Jesus by night (3:1-15); how, during a
session of the Sanhedrin, he made at least a bit of an effort to
speak up on Jesus' behalf (7:50-52); how he made a gesture of
support in bringing spices for Jesus' burial (19:39-40).

Now, if the teller of the story is himself a close colleague of
Nicodemus—namely, a second Jerusalem rabbi named Lazarus—then it could well have been Lazarus—friend of both
Jesus and Nicodemus—who set up the interview (and might
actually have been present for it). He himself could have *heard*
what Nicodemus said in the Sanhedrin meeting. It might well
have been Lazarus who superintended the burial of Jesus,

arranged the use of Arimathea's tomb, and received the spices from Nicodemus. On the other hand, if the author were John-Z, the Galilean fisherman disciple, it is hard to imagine how he would ever have come to know the inside story of Nicodemus.

Let us follow, then, this theme of the "Jewish intelligentsia" through the explicit Lazarus scenes. Bethany is just two miles from Jerusalem (11:18). Upon the death of Lazarus, "many of the Jews had come to Martha and Mary to console them" (v. 19). These Jewish leaders apparently still considered Lazarus "one of them"—even though he was, at the same time, a close friend and follower of Jesus. "When the Jews who were with her in the house, consoling her, saw Mary rise quickly and go out, they followed her" (v. 31). With great care and deliberation, the Writer is getting these Jews in place to be eyewitnesses of the raising of Lazarus (which is at the same time a type and analog of Jesus' own coming resurrection). The Writer is intent on showing that Jesus' love for, identification with, and action toward *one of their own number* is the crisis of faith that will split this Jewish community. Their obligatory choice now will be either to join Jesus or to crucify him—either to accept "the raiser of Lazarus" as himself the Resurrection and the Life or to excommunicate both Lazarus and his raiser. How they now treat their respected colleague Lazarus will be how they treat Jesus (and vice versa). And Lazarus himself is the sign that it is possible to be a follower of Jesus without renouncing the whole of Jewish intellectual culture.

"So the Jews said, 'See how he loved him!'" (v. 36). The issue is being sharpened: these Jews know that Lazarus is one of them, but at the same time they must admit that he has an especially close relationship to Jesus. Jesus declares what he is about to do and then says, "I have said this on account of the people standing by, that they may believe that thou didst send me" (v. 42). More than just an act of love for Lazarus, the raising is a challenging of Jewish intellectuals to faith (which is what the whole Fourth Gospel also is). "Many of the Jews therefore, who had come with Mary and had seen what he did, believed in him; but some of them went to the Pharisees and told them what Jesus had done" (vv. 45-46). The raising of Lazarus precludes neutrality; any Jewish intellectual must now become either a "follower" or a "crucifier" (which, again, is probably the very choice the Gospel itself is meant to present).

The Gospel's last words with Lazarus on the scene come just days later, at a supper given in Jesus' honor: "When the great crowd of the Jews learned that he was there, they came, not only on account of Jesus but also to see Lazarus, whom he had raised from the dead. So the chief priests planned to put Lazarus also to death, because on account of him many of the Jews were going away and believing in Jesus" (12:9-11).

Lazarus is close enough to Jesus that he becomes something of a "type" of Jesus himself—and thus a "type" of true discipleship. (In Synoptic-Pauline terms it would be put, "You are my body.") The threat that faces Jesus catches Lazarus. The death and raising of Lazarus is a sign of Jesus' own death and resurrection. To let oneself be loved by Jesus inevitably entails one's being caught up in the rejection that comes to him. Yet, at the same time, "on account of Lazarus" many of his Jewish colleagues came to believe in Jesus. Lazarus of Bethany, Apostle to the Jewish Intelligentsia.

The Gospel's next scene is the triumphal entry into Jerusalem, and "Lazarus" enables the Writer to make a theological point completely impossible for the Synoptic writers. Where did this welcoming crowd of Jerusalem believers and disciples come from? The Synoptics would be hard put to explain it. But the Fourth Gospel? "The crowd that had been with him when he called Lazarus out of the tomb and raised him from the dead bore witness. The reason why the crowd went to meet him was that they heard he had done this sign" (12:17-18). The person of Lazarus (in his unique dual membership both with the Jewish intelligentsia and with Jesus) and Jesus' action toward him—these actually served to trigger the polar responses of Passion Week: both the Jewish rejection represented by the crucifiers and, equally, the Jewish welcome represented by the triumphal-entry believers.

Allow me to make something of a footnote interruption and

show how identifying the author of the Fourth Gospel as
Lazarus has the effect of blunting a serious charge against and
removing a great embarrassment to the Fourth Gospel. From
time immemorial, scholars have noted this Gospel's frequent
(and almost incessant) use of the phrase "the Jews"—and that
delivered quite often in a most negative, accusatory, and even
condemnatory way. Those who have *wanted* to accuse the New
Testament of anti-Semitism have focused upon the Fourth
Gospel, and those who have tried to defend the New Testament against the charge have almost had to make an exception
of the Fourth Gospel.

Yet we now have proposed the Gospel's author to be a re-
nowned and respected Jewish rabbi-theologian-intellectual
named Lazarus. It can hardly be that such an individual would
have been anti-Semitic or that he would have intended his
term "the Jews" as a broadside against the whole of the Jewish
people. No, if the speaker is Lazarus, it follows that he is using
"the Jews" in a very specialized, circumscribed sense. He would
have known just who he had in mind—and, had the occasion
called for him to do so, he could have "fingered" them, singling
out each by name. His use of the term would be anything but a
"broadside."

"The Jews" he condemns would be colleagues from his own
intellectual and official circles—and by no means all of them.
The story of the raising itself (11:45-46) tells us that "many" of
the witnessing Jews believed but that "some" ran to the authorities. A few days later, at the supper honoring Jesus, the
account states that a "great crowd of the Jews" were on hand
because of their interest not only in Jesus but also in Lazarus.
Conversely, it is only "the chief priests" who are said to respond
by plotting to kill Lazarus as well as Jesus. And finally, at the
triumphal entry the next day, it is again the "great crowd" of
Jews that greets Jesus in friendship—by implication, only a
small clique of "the Jews" being out to get him. Clearly, Lazarus
has well protected himself against the charge of anti-Semitic
condemnation of the entire Jewish people.

The only "Jews" who give Lazarus trouble are those of his

colleagues who have always been on his back. Undoubtedly they razzed him as they had razzed Nicodemus about being a follower of Jesus: "Are you led astray, you also? Have any of the authorities or of the Pharisees believed in him?" (7:47-48). "Are you from Galilee too?" (7:52). They had probably given him a hard time about his originally joining John the Baptist, only to jump horses to Jesus (which is why he spends so much of his first chapter denying that interpretation of the matter). And the crowning insult, of course, was their being actual eyewitnesses to Jesus' ultimate revelation in raising Lazarus himself from the dead, yet their closing their eyes even to that, using it rather as an excuse to wreak their vengeance on colleague Lazarus as well as the outsider Jesus. I submit that Lazarus knew precisely who he meant by "the Jews"—and that he had excellent cause for saying what he did about them.

Of course, such accusation carries no implications regarding the Jewish people as a whole, but, given the historical evidence, I find it incredible for anyone to try to deny that there actually was a faction of Jewish authorities who were determined to get Jesus. Lazarus, the Beloved Disciple, was there—and knew what (and who) he was talking about. The effort to shift all of the blame to the Romans and deny any Jewish complicity—that just doesn't square with the facts. Neither in the Fourth Gospel nor in the Synoptics do I find any of this business of trying to finger one and only one party as GUILTY. No, the guilt is very well distributed: there *was* a contingent of Jewish authorities who wanted Jesus dead, there *was* a contingent of Roman officials who were happy to cooperate, and there *was* a contingent of Jesus' own followers who betrayed, denied, and deserted him. Jews, Gentiles, or Christians—there was no particular party of villains and no particular party of saints, either. And that's how I read Lazarus: ready to call a spade a spade when it was one, but doing so quite impartially (whether it be a Jewish dignitary, a Roman governor, or the disciple Judas—or Peter). Yet there are certainly no grounds for branding the Beloved Disciple "anti-Semitic."

Lazarus and Fourth Gospel Theology

Apart from this thematic of "Jewish faith crisis," the Lazarus scenes have some other things to tell us:

1. Notice the entirely crucial *placement* of the Lazarus story within the overall movement of the Gospel. Both as a "type" of Jesus' own death and resurrection and as a trigger of the polar responses of Jewish acceptance/rejection of Jesus, the story serves as a bridge between Jesus' public ministry and his culminating work of Passion Week. Lazarus stands as the disciple-pivot around whom the Gospel is organized; not even Peter has that sort of honor in this particular Gospel.

2. One little exchange in the midst of the Lazarus story well typifies the nature of the relationship between the Synoptic theology of historical eschatology and the Fourth Gospel theology of divine communication: "Jesus said to her, 'Your brother will rise again.' Martha said to him, 'I know that he will rise again in the resurrection at the last day.' Jesus said to her, 'I am the resurrection and the life; he who believes in me, though he die, yet shall he live, and whoever lives and believes in me shall never die'" (11:23-26).

When Martha refers to Lazarus's rising at the last day—as part of the general, cosmic resurrection of the world at the end of history (a new heaven and a new earth)—this clearly puts her in the thought world of historical eschatology. The response of the Fourth Gospel Jesus (speaking in a way the Synoptic Jesus never does) just as clearly puts him in the thought world of divine communication: Jesus *is* immediately the resurrection and the life for whoever chooses to believe at whatever moment—without regard to world history, the time-scale of its destiny, or the believer's place and role within that development.

Here, as at a number of other points in the Fourth Gospel, the Writer says enough to show that he is aware of and understands the eschatological way of thinking. He understands it, but he isn't ready to buy into it; yet neither does he show any desire to deny, rebut, or combat it. Rather, as here, he simply passes it over in favor of his own way of doing theology.

The issue is not the simple distinction between a future-oriented faith and a present-oriented one; the issue, rather, is *how* the present benefits of Christ are to be understood and interpreted. Mainline biblical eschatology (a) wants to keep even the benefits of present experience rooted *historically,* as public effects manifest in the life of the Christian community (or even the larger society) and in the lives of individuals precisely as they participate in historical community; and (b) wants always to interpret present benefits *in light of* that future consummation by seeing them as foretastes, premonitions, promises, and guarantees of the ultimate benefits of the yet-to-come kingdom of God. In short, historical eschatology sees "present benefits" always as pointing beyond themselves, while divine communication sees them as ends in themselves.

On the other hand, the answer that the Fourth Gospel Jesus gives to Martha is a beautiful specimen of the theology of divine communication. World history and its course aren't even in the picture. Rather, we have what technically would be called "realized eschatology." At whatever point in time since Christ's death and resurrection, any and all of his benefits already have been communicated and are as immediately available to the believer as they ever have been or ever will be. There is no reason to refer anything to the future, because all the gifts and benefits of eschatological promise have already been "realized" in Christ.

And notice that the recipient of this divine communication is himself inevitably "de-historicized" and "de-communitized" as the subject of private, individualized blessing. "He who believes in me" (namely, whatever individual chooses to believe at whatever time), "he" (and only he) shall have communicated "to him" *eternal life*—"even though *he* die, yet shall *he* live."

My own opinion is that divine communication is great stuff—if it is supplemented with strong doses of historical eschatology (the New Testament's own proportioning, of course,

Lazarus = Another Disciple = The Beloved Disciple/Mary-L = Mary Magdalene

John THE CALL 1:35-42	RAISING 10:40-11:55	ANOINTING 12:1-11	TRIUMPHAL ENTRY vv. 12-19	DISCOURSE vv. 20-50	LAST SUPPER 13:1-38	JESUS' TRIAL 18:15-18
Andrew & another disciple of J.B. leave him to follow Jesus	Lazarus raised about a week before Passover at Bethany	Lazarus named as present six days before Passover at Bethany	Lazarus named as involved		Bel. Disc. closer to Jesus than Peter is	Another disciple gets Peter in
	Mary-L active in the story	Mary-L anoints Jesus				

Mark 1:16-20		14:3-9	11:1-10		14:17-25	14:53-72
Simon, Andrew, James, & John called as Galilean fishermen		"a woman" anoints Jesus at Bethany, in the house of Simon, before Passover	no Lazarus		names no disciples	Peter is by himself

Matthew 4:18-22		26:6-13	21:1-11		26:20-29	26:57-75
same as Mark		same as Mark	no Lazarus		names only Judas	Peter is by himself

Luke 5:1-11	10:38-42	7:36-8:1	19:28-40		22:14-23	22:54-62
story of miraculous catch/fails to name Andrew among first four	much earlier than in John, Jesus visits Mary & Martha	early in Jesus' career/at Simon's house; no town named/story greatly changed/woman called "a sinner"/ Mary M. (of 7 demons) named immediately following	no Lazarus		names no disciples	Peter is by himself

Read John horizontally to get his picture; then read vertically to see what sort

Lazarus = Another Disciple = The Beloved Disciple/Mary-L = Mary Magdalene

AT THE CROSS 19:25-27	JESUS' BURIAL 19:38-42	EMPTY TOMB 20:1-2	EMPTY TOMB vv. 3-10	EMPTY TOMB vv. 11-18	SEASHORE 21:4-8	SEASHORE vv. 9-24
Bel. Disc. called "son of Jesus' mother"	Joseph of Arimathea and Nicodemus involved	"The other disciple, the one whom Jesus loved" & Peter get the word	Bel. Disc. outruns Peter to the tomb	After Bel. Disc. & Peter have gone home	Bel. Disc. tells Peter that the stranger is Jesus	Jesus tells Peter not to concern himself with fate of Bel. Disc.
Mary Magdalene present	no women	Mary Magdalene (solo) brings that word	Mary M. comes behind	Mary M. has intimate scene with Jesus		

15:40-41	15:42-47	16:1-8	16:9-10 (long ending)
Mary M. and other women "looking on from afar"	Joseph A., Mary M., and one other woman	Mary M. and other women instructed to go tell his disciples and Peter	Mary M., from whom Jesus had cast out seven demons, was first to whom he appeared and the one who *did* tell disciples

27:55-56	27:57-61	28:1-10
Mary M. but different "others"	same as Mark	Mary M. with different list of women

23:49	23:50-56	24:1-12
unnamed "acquaintances & women"	Joseph A. and unnamed women	Mary M. with still different list of women

of support he gets from the Synoptics.

is three parts Synoptics to one part Fourth Gospel). Yet, if it be taken as standing alone, I'm not sure it is adequate as a Christian theology—nor can it be said to be fully *biblical*.

And for our present purposes, the point of our exegeting John 11:23-26 is this: If (as surely is the case) the Beloved Disciple is the source not only of the Fourth Gospel memories of Jesus but of the Fourth Gospel theology as well, then (both because of his connections with Jewish intellectualism and for the fact that the theology of divine communication is written right into his story) Lazarus certainly qualifies as a better candidate for the Beloved Disciple than John-Z ever could.

Do "Lazarus and Sister Mary" Equal "Beloved Disciple and Mary Magdalene"?

We are now ready to try Lazarus as the Beloved Disciple *outside* the specific Lazarus scenes. The accompanying chart graphically lays out the data; the remainder of our study will involve little more than following it through. We can use the chart now as something of an overview and outline. Once our study is complete, the chart may be even more valuable for purposes of summary and review.

The Fourth Gospel gives us two (and only two) unique great disciple figures: Lazarus and the Beloved Disciple (with whom, out of the Synoptic tradition, only Peter would begin to compare). The Fourth Gospel duo do not *overlap*—thank heavens! If they did—if they were to appear side by side in a single scene—that would completely blow our theory. However, it is amazing how close they come to linking up. Let's get them properly located.

As we have seen, the Writer of the Fourth Gospel must have found it all-important to get his Beloved Disciple's induction into discipleship written into the opening of the book. Yet it is evident that he had no desire to introduce either the Beloved Disciple or Lazarus into the action of that phase. Consequently, it is not surprising that neither of them appears be-

fore the midpoint. That first half of the Gospel covers pre-
dominantly Jesus' Galilean ministry (the milieu of the Twelve),
and there is no likelihood that Lazarus (or the Beloved Disciple) was even around. So it is only with chapter 11, precisely
with the Writer's move into the Jerusalem half of his book,
precisely with Jesus entering his Passion, that LAZARUS is
introduced to play what we have seen is a most crucial and
significant role. Though named only in this single, two-chap-
ter passage, Lazarus is not simply a passing character but a
structural element of the Gospel.

He has the featured role, of course, in the account of Jesus'
raising him. He then is named as present at the supper where
his sister Mary anoints Jesus for burial. In the account of the
triumphal entry of the next day, Lazarus is named as making
the event possible, though not necessarily as being present.
With this, in the middle of chapter 12, all mention of Lazarus
ceases. The latter half of chapter 12, then, is almost totally
discourse with no real action involved. Chapter 13 opens with
the Last Supper in the upper room—and here, for the very
first time, big as life, lying upon the breast of Jesus, is the
BELOVED DISCIPLE. And from this point on he appears in
almost every major scene to the end of the book. There is no
overlap or (perhaps) any explicit link between Lazarus and the
Beloved Disciple, yet these two figures together effectively
cover, give continuity to, and tie together the entire Jeru-
salem/Passion Week half of the Gospel.

And there *would* be a very nice and very convincing link *if* it
could be shown that the Writer considers Lazarus's sister Mary
(hereafter Mary-L) and Mary Magdalene to be the same woman. But that's a tough one to settle either way. However, if they
are meant to be the same woman, then the Fourth Gospel has
Mary (with her sister Martha) at the raising of brother Lazarus.
Next, still in the company of her brother and sister, she anoints
Jesus for his burial. Next (now called Mary Magdalene) she is
at the cross, still with her brother (if he be the Beloved Disciple). And finally, she is the discoverer of the empty tomb who

runs to tell her brother (if he be the Beloved Disciple) and Peter. If Mary-L and Mary Magdalene are one person, then her story does move directly from Lazarus to the Beloved Disciple and proves that they are one person, too.

The problem: Mary-L is found only in the Fourth Gospel and in Luke. Luke 10:38-42 names Mary and her sister Martha, though without naming their "village." This much is certainly a confirmation of Mary-L's historicity, but because Luke shows no knowledge of a brother Lazarus, he can't provide much in the way of hard evidence.

All four Gospels have the account of a woman anointing Jesus with precious ointment and agree on enough detail and language to suggest that they are all telling the same story. However, in this case it is Luke (rather than the Fourth Gospel) that is the maverick, making the whole matter problematic again. With the exception of Luke, all the Gospels locate the incident at *Bethany* on the eve of, or during, *Passion Week,* and make the anointing proleptic of *the burial of Jesus.* Only the Fourth Gospel names the woman—and that as Mary-L. But if that evangelist was himself present in the person of Lazarus and is talking about his own sister, he, of course, is the one in the best position to say who she was. The concurrence of Mark and Matthew regarding other details of the account put them in support of her identification as Mary-L.

Luke *does* know of Mary-L (and her sister Martha) but tells the anointing story in a way that puts it entirely at odds with the three other accounts. He places the story much earlier in Jesus' career (7:36-50), drops the Bethany location and the reference to Jesus' burial, and changes the story to give it an entirely different point. Our first impulse might be to say that it isn't even the same story—though we will find enough clues to indicate that Luke knew it was.

In the first place, Luke's phrase "an alabaster flask of ointment" (7:37) is identical, word for word, with what he would have found in Mark 14:3.

Second, Mark says the anointing took place in the Bethany house of "Simon the leper," and Luke has Jesus addressing his host as "Simon" (a remarkable coincidence indeed, if two different anointings both involved "an alabaster flask of ointment" and happened in the houses of two different men named "Simon").

Third, although Luke's account coincides in these ways with the Synoptic Mark-Matthew account, it also coincides in one amazing way with the *Fourth Gospel* version of the story. Mark and Matthew agree that the woman anointed Jesus' *head*. Yet Luke deliberately disregards his Markan source on that point in order to agree instead with the Beloved Disciple that she anointed his *feet* and then dried them *with her hair*. Luke apparently knows *both* versions of the story and combines them.

In the fourth place, I find evidence that Luke himself did not think there had been two different anointings. When it moves into its account of Passion Week, the Gospel of Mark speaks of the plotting against Jesus in 14:1-2, and here Luke follows Mark very closely, as Luke 22:1-2 shows. With verse 3 of chapter 14, Mark launches into the anointing story (vv. 3-9), and when it is completed, with verse 10 he begins his account of Judas's betrayal. And lo and behold, Luke's verses 3-4 of chapter 22 are almost identical to Mark's verse 10. What Luke has done is to follow Mark right up through the verse immediately preceding mention of the anointing, skip the anointing, and then pick up again with Mark's first verse after his recounting of the anointing. Now why would Luke do that—unless he knew he had already used that anointing story and so ought not to duplicate it here? If he considered them to be two entirely different events, he would have no good reason for skipping Mark's account of the second one. I think it is clear that Luke's anointing story is the same story found in the other three Gospels—a story that Luke moved and adapted for his own purposes of theological teaching (understanding those purposes as taking priority over the preservation of precise historical detail).

Yet, although it is different, Luke's anointing story may preserve some valuable information. He does not name the woman (any more than the other Synoptics do), but he does make the unique specification that she was "a woman of the city, who was a sinner" (which we ought not to read automatically as meaning "prostitute," there being any number of other possibilities). Then, immediately following the anointing story, in the unique passage of 8:1-3, Luke names some women who traveled with Jesus—including "Mary, called Magdalene, from whom seven demons had gone out" (which, by the way, would well qualify her as "a woman of the city, who was a sinner"—good people certainly not finding themselves cursed with demon possession). Is Luke hinting that Mary Magdalene was the sinful woman who had done the anointing?

That is a distinct possibility, because—in this case too— Luke is busy shifting things around. Here he *says* nothing about Mary Magdalene that he couldn't have derived from Mark. Where Luke 8:2 reads "Mary, called Magdalene, from whom seven demons had gone out," Mark 16:9 has "Mary Magdalene, from whom he [Jesus] had cast out seven demons." The difference is that Mark (along with the other Gospel writers except Luke) introduces Mary Magdalene only at the cross. The bit about her demon possession comes even later, in Mark's long ending of 16:9-20. So Luke's information on Mary Magdalene—as well as his anointing story—involved major displacements of his Markan material. Can it be sheer accident that the two "moved pieces" (i.e., the account of the woman anointing Jesus and the information about Mary Magdalene) landed in the same place, one hard up against the other?

The Writer of the Fourth Gospel explicitly names Lazarus's sister Mary-L as the anointing woman. Luke already has shown himself to know at least something of Fourth Gospel tradition and of the existence of Mary-L (which is not the case with the other Synoptists)—and he comes close to agreeing that the anointing woman was named "Mary" (though "Mary Magdalene" in his case). However, if Mary-L and Mary Magdalene are the same person, both Luke and the Fourth Gospel could be right.

The further treatment of Mary Magdalene is remarkably consistent in all four Gospels. In different ways, all four of the Gospels designate women as present, first at the cross and then at the garden tomb. But of all the women named, Mary Magdalene is the only one on which there is unanimous agreement. Otherwise, it is pretty much a case of each writer's women being different from everyone else's. Mary Magdalene is the only one of whom we can speak with certainty. And the Fourth Gospel's account is the only one making a claim to be that of an eyewitness. It is the only account that has a man (a male) present—the Beloved Disciple, of course (with 19:35 insisting that he is the eyewitness who has told the truth of the matter).

Mark next has Mary Magdalene among the women at the entombment of Jesus. Matthew again agrees. Luke again has women there but does not name them. The Fourth Gospel entombment scene names only Joseph of Arimathea and Nicodemus and doesn't involve women.

Mark finally has Mary Magdalene among the women at the tomb on Easter morning, and the longer ending of that Gospel gives her some priority as a witness of the Resurrection. Matthew follows Mark in having her there, but does not give her any particular priority. Luke agrees that Magdalene was present, but on this occasion names *more* women than the other Gospel writers, though without giving particular priority to Mary. The Fourth Gospel also has Mary Magdalene present, yet in a role different enough to call for special consideration.

Here, Mary plays the tomb scene solo; there is no hint that any other women are present. She discovers the empty tomb and runs to tell Peter and the Beloved Disciple. The two race back to the tomb, and she apparently comes along behind. Presumably while the two men are in the tomb (or after they have left the place), she has a most special and intimate conversation with the risen Lord, whom she mistakes for the gardener. This scene is such that it is quite reminiscent of the earlier accounts in the Fourth Gospel and in Luke of the intimacy between Jesus and Mary-L. And finally, it is Mary Magdalene's privilege to carry the news of the Resurrection to the "disciples" (which, in the Fourth Gospel, might designate either the Galilean Twelve or a larger, mixed group).

When we put it all together, obviously there is nothing that adds up to a *positive* identification of Mary-L as Mary Magdalene. But on the other hand, neither is anything said that would in any way *prohibit,* or even discourage, the identification. For instance, if Jesus sometime earlier had cast seven demons out of Mary-L, that would serve only to explain and accentuate the intimacy of their friendship.

So, I find four subtle hints that Mary-L and Mary Magdalene are to be considered the same person:

1. The anointing woman that the Fourth Gospel positively identifies as "Mary-L" Luke may know as "Mary Magdalene."

2. Mary-L would fit very naturally into every scene the Fourth Gospel gives Mary Magdalene—particularly if, at the cross, it is the case that Lazarus and his sister Mary are offering Jesus' mother a home in Bethany. (This makes more sense than reading the scene as if the Fourth Gospel, of all books, is having John-Z—who likely wasn't even there—take her off to Galilee.)

3. The scene with Jesus and Mary Magdalene in the garden as much as asks to be read in continuity with the scene of Jesus and Mary-L at Bethany (and the other Jesus/Mary scene in Luke).

4. Perhaps the strongest clue of all is the situation the chart makes graphic—namely, that the Fourth Gospel has carefully paired a Mary (Mary-L) with its LAZARUS in certain episodes and thereafter paired a Mary (Mary Magdalene) with its BELOVED DISCIPLE in certain episodes. This pattern could hardly be coincidental; it must be an effort to tell us *something*.

Lazarus in the Beloved Disciple Role

With "Mary" on file, then, as supporting evidence, let's see how "Lazarus" works as an identity for the disciple whom Jesus loved:

At the Last Supper (John 13): If it is John-Z who is lying on Jesus' breast and with whom even Peter must confer to get to Jesus, this suggests favoritism that could produce jealousy among the Twelve and could cause trouble among those who have just inadmissibly been fighting for power among themselves. However, if that disciple is the man who, just a matter of days earlier, Jesus had raised from the dead, and if he were no one who ever had or ever would live and travel with the Twelve in any case, then my guess is that everyone present would have been eager to have him in the place of special honor, perhaps even willing to address him as "the disciple whom Jesus loves."

In the courtyard of the high priest (18:12-27): Considering the high level of Jewish connections that this Gospel attributes to Lazarus, it is not surprising that he knew the high priest and could walk right into the court where Jesus was being tried—and had enough influence to get Peter in, too. However, it is a little hard to believe that the Galilean fisherman John-Z could have pulled this off.

At the cross (19:23-37): It is plausible to read this scene as showing Lazarus and his sister Mary—in the company of Jerusalem women—offering Jesus' mother a home in Bethany, with Jesus naming this very special individual (rather than any one member out of his Galilean group) as the son of his mother. This makes much better sense—particularly in the Fourth Gospel—than having John-Z in the role, especially when the Synoptics indicate that the Galilean Twelve had all fled.

At the empty tomb (20:1-18): That Mary should run to tell her brother Lazarus *and* Peter about Jesus, and that the two of them should *race* each other to the tomb—such a scenario fits the Fourth Gospel pattern of "Jerusalem discipleship *and* Galilean discipleship" to a T. If, however, the scene is read such that Mary tells John-Z and Peter about Christ, and *they* race to the tomb, the scene carries no symbolic significance at all, since those two men represent the same thing.

With the risen Christ on the seashore (John 21): Recall that this chapter is the special appendix that seems to have been added to follow the Gospel's original conclusion. That means this scene is already somewhat set apart from the others. And, in terms of *historical plausibility,* I admit that it isn't easy to fit Lazarus into this scene—into a fishing boat on the Sea of Galilee. John-Z would be much more of a natural for this one. However, if this chapter is read as a *theological construction,* its latter half becomes the strongest pointer to Lazarus that could be found. And because the Writer's primary interest throughout the Gospel has been theological construction, here we should probably go with a "Lazarus reading" and handle the historical plausibility as best we can.

In the "feed my sheep" dialogue (vv. 15-19), Jesus commissions Peter—and through him, the Galilean Twelve—to the great apostolate that subsequently proceeded from them. Yet when, in verses 20ff., Peter turns to ask, "Lord, what about this man [Lazarus]?" Jesus in effect responds, "That's no business of yours, Peter. You have your assignment, and I will do with Lazarus and his 'apostolate to the Jerusalem intelligentsia' as I choose."

But consider those named in the whole of Gospel tradition; would there be any reason for a "saying" about "not dying" to attach itself to any of them except Lazarus? Only he is both the disciple about whom it is explicitly said that Jesus loved him and the one whose very existence was owed to Jesus' miraculous communication of a special quality of life people might easily assume could have no end. And when the Writer takes such pains to get the saying understood correctly, does this not imply that, by the time of the writing of this Gospel (the writing of at least this last, added chapter), Lazarus actually had died? And would not the Writer then need to assure people that Lazarus's death did not invalidate the fact that he nevertheless was "the disciple whom Jesus loved"? Jesus never said that this living miracle, having already died once, would never have to die again; that was a misunderstanding. So, what sense would verses 23-24 make if that disciple were actually John-Z (or, for that matter, anyone other than the singular Lazarus)?

I am not claiming here to have *proved* that Lazarus of Bethany was the Beloved Disciple. But I will say again that, if it is not Lazarus, then we have not been given a ghost of an idea about who it might have been. Lazarus fits better than any other possible candidate.

NOTE: I'm sorry. I realize that this theory only adds to the burden of "liberal" scholars who already have their hands full trying to get around the bodily resurrection of Jesus. Here, now, we have a Writer solemnly averring that he got his account of the raising of Lazarus not via an extended oral church tradition but directly from the mouth of the person who claimed to be not simply an eyewitness but the very subject of the raising itself. "This is the disciple who is bearing witness to these things, and who has caused these things to be written; and we know his testimony is true."

Study Two

The Beloved Disciple: His Thought

As we turn now to spot and then explore what may be the central insight of the Fourth Gospel, nothing demands that we identify the Beloved Disciple as Lazarus. Feel very free to either accept or reject this idea. However, it will be *helpful* to continue thinking of that Beloved Disciple as a Jewish rabbi/scholar with much more education and sophistication than is represented by the Galilean Twelve.

It will quickly become apparent that the frame of reference for this study is what we earlier designated as the Fourth Gospel's "divine communication" (how it is that God's blessing can be communicated from his sphere of "the eternal heavenly" and made accessible to us in our sphere of "the earthly sinful"). The surprise will be that the Fourth Gospel itself deliberately contradicts what the church has regularly understood to be the Fourth Gospel's own answer. The communication happens through anything but human religious experience—what the old hymn ("The Church's One Foundation") calls "mystic sweet communion."

Actually, we will discover, the Beloved Disciple is taking a bead on the total phenomenon we call "Christendom"—as that has existed from his own day in the first century right down to ours in the twentieth. However, in his crucial passages the "Christendom issue" is focused on the particular question of "sacrament," and even more particularly on the matter of the

Eucharist, the bread and cup of the Lord's Supper. So it seems wise for us to run our argument the other way: start with "sacrament" and show how that characterizes Christendom at large. Eventually, then, we will bring the Beloved Disciple back into the act.

SACRAMENT AS "MYSTERY" THINKING

The only way to begin now is with a careful scrutiny of that word "sacrament." It is a Latin derivation built upon a root referring to a pledge or an oath and carrying strong overtones of the sacred or holy. Most significant, the Latin "sacrament" is successor and close equivalent to the Greek word "mystery"— the two words carrying much the same sense.

The Greek predecessor "mystery" *is* used a number of times in the New Testament, although never in reference to (or even in conjunction with) baptism or the Lord's Supper. Also, these New Testament occurrences consistently lack any note of appreciating mystery for its own sake, any attributing of religious significance to the human sense of mystery. Indeed, regularly (and perhaps even invariably) the gospel is valued precisely for the fact that it demystifies "mystery." This is indicated throughout the New Testament by the terms accompanying the word "mystery": "been given to know," "made known," "make all men see," "understand," "insight into," "now disclosed," "I tell you," "impart," "proclaim." Most typical is Colossians 1:26 with its reference to "the mystery hidden for ages and generations but now made manifest to his saints." Completely contrary to the "sacramental" interpretation, Scripture values "mystery" only in its ceasing to be mysterious.

What this means, then, is that Scripture played no part in Christendom's decision that its baptism and Supper should be called "sacraments." That wasn't done even in *reference* to Scripture, let alone in an effort to be biblical. It was a later decision made by the church on its own—and, I think, largely under the extra-Christian influences of paganism. Clearly, both before Christ and since, "world religions" have been very much given to ideas of mystery and sacrament. These have always been understood as the proper modes for "divine communication."

Yet, unfortunately, the word "sacrament" does serve as a quite accurate description of what the church proceeded also to *make* of baptism and the Supper—namely, matters of "mystery" and "mystical experience." And it is not just baptism and the Supper that have been treated so. Right down to the present day we can trace Christendom's tendency to "mysticize" that faith which the New Testament originally presented in totally demystified form.

We need here to define "mysticism" in the broadest possible terms, so I am using it to denote "that which human agents have it in their power to do in the way of putting themselves into contact with, and gaining some experience of, the transcendent mystery of life and all being." Notice particularly that the mystical approach is not at all interested in "breaking" mystery—in fathoming it or having it revealed so that it is no longer mysterious. Quite the opposite. Mystery is here approached precisely that it might be enjoyed—and that one might be edified and enriched by it. It is only *as mystery* (as mystic experience) that it amounts to "divine communication."

The human hunger for mystery seems to be culturally and religiously universal, though we now mean to confine our attention to Christian mysticism—that is, those forms of mysticism appearing within the Christian church and its tradition. "Sacramentalism" is just one of these forms, and we need to develop the broader context in the process of getting at this one type. The listing to follow will run from the "higher" forms (more sophisticated and elitist) to the "lower" forms (more everyday and garden variety). And our conclusion will be that New Testament Christianity is in basic opposition to any and all moves toward "mysticism."

Intellectualist Mysticism (Gnosis): We here refer to the penchant that at least begins with those philosophers and philosophic theologians (among whom the Beloved Disciple is regularly included) dedicated to *explaining* Christianity in the intellectualist terminology of systematic reason, conceptualization, and idea. Invariably, the first move is to reconceptualize "God" *away* from the quite specific, down-to-earth, anthropomorphic, and what are considered "primitive" metaphors in which Scripture presents him. The intellectualist way, rather, is to define him (or "it") in terms that are ever more general, abstract, theoretical, specious, ambiguous, esoteric, ethereal, *mysterious,* and unbiblical.

The move is underway when even ordinary, non-intellectualist Christians (including pastors) show a preference for addressing or describing God in the grandiose (but empty of specific content) language of liturgy: "World Spirit," "Creator," "Power of Love," "Ultimate Reality," "Light," "the Eternal," "the Word" *(Logos),* etc. (I have deliberately included some Fourth Gospel usages that we will want to come back to.) And, of course, the current feminist insistence that no gendered language be used for God—this only aggravates the tendency.

However, among the philosophic theologians themselves, the move is that of extending intellectual comprehension as far as it will go—always pushing "God" ahead and into the incomprehensibility that lies just beyond. Most often, that which is just beyond comprehension is indicated by calling God "Being" (though never "a being," which specificity lies on the wrong side of the line), "Being Itself," or "the Ground of Being." And the first thing to be noted about these terms is that they refer to sheer mystery, that about which nothing whatever can be said. If one were capable of saying anything specific about "Being," it would not be the highest concept possible. An idea about which "nothing" can be said (because it transcends thought, understanding, and experience) is obviously a higher idea than one about which "something" can be said.

To call God "Being" is to identify God (and here one dare

not use a personal pronoun or even an impersonal one), but it is to identify God as sheer and utter mystery. Indeed, "God" is now *categorical* mystery—which to "break" or to "reveal" would be, in effect, to ruin as God. And for proponents of this school of Christian thought, religious experience (divine communication) consists in our sense of confronting "Being Itself," finding ourselves acceptable to Being and accepted by Being. Yet that very experience will have to be as mysterious as all get-out. Even the language used to describe it must, of necessity, be more specific-anthropomorphic than actually suits the case. My "being accepted" (in any truly human sense of the phrase) assumes a person-to-person relationship that simply cannot be made to apply to "Being Itself" (about which nothing specific dare be said, remember).

Although most of modern theology stops short of this God of Being (God as Ultimate Religious Mystery), the theological trend of our day clearly is to move *away* from the Bible's quite specific God (who even bears the proper name "Yahweh") and *toward* the mystery of abstraction and theoretical idea. Nevertheless, Karl Barth argues directly against this stream in his exposition of the Lord's Prayer in *The Christian Life:*

Father as a vocative, whether expressed or not, is the primal form of the thinking, the primal sound of the speaking, and the primal act of the obedience demanded of Christians. . . . This word gives the required precision, the appropriate fullness, and the authentic interpretation to a word that in itself is indefinite, empty, and ambivalent, namely, the word "God." God himself, the one true and real God, obviously does not need this in order to avoid indistinctness, emptiness, and ambivalence. But the word "God" in all human languages does need it, for it can mean everything for some, this or that for others, and even nothing at all, or a mere illusion, for others. (Pp. 51, 53)

Here, where intellectualist mysticism wants to take the word "God" still further to the left, Barth insists that, for the Bible, even the word "God" is not good enough but must itself be taken further right. And it should be pointed out that, on this point, Jesus was even more of a rightist than Karl Barth. When the disciples asked Jesus how they should pray to God, according to Luke 11:2—which stands the best chance of having it right—Jesus responded, "Just call him 'Father'—anything fancier than that is a showing off of your religion, not a glorifying of him." And some scholars think that, in the mouth of Jesus, even that "Father" was actually "Abba" (the Aramaic "Dear Daddy" term that is about as simple and down-to-earth as one can get). I think Barth is correct about Scripture's aversion to "divine mystery," and so, in a bit, I will let the Beloved Disciple (of all people) clinch the case.

If to move toward mystery is this unbiblical, why should Christendom always want to be doing so? What is the tendency, the motive pulling things in this direction? I don't know that I have the full answer, but let me try the insight I have: The more specific, close, real, down-to-earth, and personal God is, the better is his position for exercising his particular functions of lordship, authority, judgment, command, discipline, counsel, and direction—as also his particular functions of love, grace, forgiveness, resurrection, and salvation (very much "person" terms, one and all). Conversely, the further God is pushed into the passive realm of mystery, the more room that leaves us to take over as our own lords, authorities, and counselors—and at the same time, to eliminate any need for grace or forgiveness (there being no one there who could call us guilty in the first place).

The device is what is known as "kicking the boss upstairs." By *promoting* God to the realm of awe, adoration, and mystery, we effectively get him off our backs. Certainly I need have no fear that a God of Pure Being (about which nothing specific can be said) can get itself specific enough to demand anything specific of *me*—or to express untoward opinions of me and my behavior. A God of Mystery is the easiest possible divinity to live with.

We need at some point (and no better spot than here) to interrupt ourselves long enough to make clear that there is a Christian use of the term "mystery" lying entirely outside the present argument. Time after time, of course, the thoughts of God and the ways of God run quite beyond our comprehension. Thus, for instance, it is perfectly proper to suggest that it is a real "mystery" that God has loved us while we were yet sinners. Technically, that isn't even an identification of God with "mystery"; it's an admission of our own limited comprehension. Yet, more significantly, it is by no means a suggestion that "God" is "mystery itself"—namely, a concept totally unspecific, devoid of cognitive content, one about which nothing can be said. Not at all; regarding the mysterious love of God, there are a great number of very specific things that can be said. The only problem is that there is so much cognitive content that the human mind is swamped by it. Clearly, our present critique of "mysticism" has no intention of being negative toward this other (and biblical) concept of "mystery."

Ecstatic Mysticism: This form is still highly specialized, though not necessarily on the basis of intellectuality. It names the classic type commonly referred to as "mysticism," the practitioners of which are known as "the mystics." In this case, "God" is approached much more *experientially* than *intellectually* (as with our previous class). "God" is that which is *experienced* as the culmination of one's highly prescribed and disciplined program of devotion, meditation, and spiritual ascension. Many of the classic mystics may also have had close, everyday communion with the "specified" Dear Daddy of Scripture—but that, if we may say so, came to them through avenues other than their mystical experience.

When the mystics describe their mystical exaltation, their accounts of God are very much couched in terms of "mystery." Their interior experience is highly valued as spiritual ecstasy—an altered state of consciousness often described as a merging into God, a losing of one's own sense of self-identity, a becoming one with God. Yet the God into whom they merge is hardly identifiable as that very much specified God of the Bible. The mystics usually come away from an experience without being able to share any cognitive content, any insight about who God is or what is his specific will or command. The God of the mystics is, for the most part, as incomprehensible, impersonal, and nonspecific as that of the gnosis-seeking intellectuals. Through their techniques of spirituality, these people approach the Ineffable Mystery and then come away with the Mystery just as ineffable as it was to start with.

The current, again, flows directly contrary to that of the New Testament. That document—with its strong emphasis upon "by their fruits you shall know them"—shows no particular interest in programmed spiritual disciplines pointed toward ecstasies of inner experience. And its most relevant comment is probably Paul's opinion on "mysteries in the Spirit":

For one who speaks in a tongue speaks not to men but to God; for no one understands him, but he utters mysteries in the Spirit. On the other hand, he who prophesies speaks to men for their upbuilding and encouragement and consolation. . . . So with yourselves; since you are eager for manifestations of the Spirit, strive to excel in building up the church. (1 Cor. 14:2-3, 12)

However, Paul's most effective treatment of "mysticism" is probably 2 Corinthians 12:1-10. Clearly, at this point in time Paul had had about as much as he could take of smart-aleck Corinthian Christians claiming grandiose mystical experiences. So, if boasting was to be the name of the game, he could outboast them without half trying. Why, he knew a guy (himself, as it turned out) who, as long as fourteen years ago (before the Corinthians had even heard of Christianity), had been caught up to the third heaven, where he had heard things that cannot be told, which man may not utter. (Paul nicely supports our point about the ineffability, the *fruitless incommunicability* of divine mystery *as mystery*.)

So Paul could be (and had been) as mystical as the best of

them. Yet he had never talked about it, never encouraged his people in that direction, would not have brought up the matter now except for having been goaded into it. And why not? Because such experience is of no particular Christian value. Indeed, the one consequence Paul attributes to his "abundance of revelations" is that they got him "too elated," got him thinking too highly of himself. And so, in order to correct Paul's spiritual misuse of ecstatic experience, God had to harass him with a thorn in the flesh, a messenger from Satan.

And (read Paul carefully here) he says that that ornery thorn proved a much more effective vehicle of "divine communication" than all his mystical experience put together. He never claims that any positive "fruit" has come from spiritual ecstasy *as ecstasy,* though he does not deny that, on occasion, ecstasy has *accompanied* content-bearing communications from God. But the measure of Christian experience *has* to be the "cognitive content" involved and not the degree of "spiritual thrill." Accordingly, the "fruit" of his thorn experience was a very specific and practical insight—namely, the understanding that, in the depth of our human weakness, the grace of God is wonderfully sufficient in bringing us through and making us strong. And of course, this was a fruit that Paul could (and did) share all over the place and put to very good use in the building up of the church. But the New Testament never promotes mystical experience as a value in and of itself.

Peak-Experience Mysticism: This may be nothing more than the amateur, "anybody can do it" version of the mysticism just discussed. The concept and practice, we will discover, is pervasive in Christendom—though I am here pegging the *theory* to the researches of a widely influential psychologist of religion, Abraham Maslow. Being a scientist, Maslow set out to present a *scientific* description of religion.

His first premise was that, whether the subject be Christianity, other of the world religions, or even secular and unformulated faiths, they all represent the one phenomenon of "human religiousness," and therefore one can properly do analysis without discriminating between them. "Christianity" is one way of doing religion; "Islam" is a variant form for doing the same thing.

Maslow's second premise was that scientifically, of course, there are no data enabling an investigator even to have an opinion about whether there actually exists a God, a god, a divine being, or anything else superior to the sphere of scientifically verifiable reality. Accordingly, the study of religion dare not even address that question but must confine itself to the human phenomenon—namely, to what human subjects say religiousness feels like and what it does for them.

Given Maslow's chosen parameters, it is not surprising that he should come to the conclusion that "religion" consists wholly and solely in the psychology of what he calls "peak experiences" and that the significance of these experiences lies entirely in the subject's internal feeling about them. Because no consideration can be given to "objective content" (for instance, to whether the subject spoke meaningfully and truly when he said he had been filled by the Holy Spirit), the only possible measure is the subject's testimony that he experienced an altered state of consciousness he would call "peak." And in Maslow's judgment all peak experiences are religiously the same—no matter how they are induced or with what mythical content the subject imbues them.

If you will, then, notice how close a "peak experience of disregarded cognitive content" comes to what we have been calling "mystery." Whatever an individual happens to believe about divine agencies causing or communicating themselves in his experience—all that is entirely incidental, the one reality being the "mystery" of his altered state of consciousness.

According to Maslow, "religiousness" is a constant and universal factor in our human makeup. There is absolutely no room for talking about "true religion" and "false religion." Everyone by nature is equally religious—the only possible distinction being that what we ordinary people call "peak experiences" the mystic specialists of our former categories would know to be only molehills.

Yet, for Maslow, "God" has now become so mysterious as to be nonexistent. Scientifically, of course, Maslow does not (and cannot) outlaw the very possibility of God's existence. What he does do is argue that the question of whether or not God exists does not affect human religiousness either one way or another. If we *believe* that a God exists, that belief can be as effective for inducing our peak experiences as his actual existence and presence would be; his actuality would give us nothing we don't already have. So this God who maybe is and maybe is not (no matter either way) is as mysterious as can be. And "religion as peak experience" is of a piece with our other mysticisms that move God (even Yahweh) away from his biblical specificity and leftward into the realm of the vague, impersonal, and mysterious.

My impression is that there are comparatively few theologians who publicly identify themselves as being both Christians and followers of Maslow; that would constitute too plain and obvious a contradiction. At the same time, I think there are many contemporary liberal theologians who—if they be carefully read and attended to—will be found intimating this very contradiction (i.e., suggesting that religion is an entirely human phenomenon to which the existence of a biblically specific God is completely optional). It is not for me to say whether these thinkers simply have failed to see what they are doing or whether theirs is a deliberate effort to undermine biblical Christianity.

However, my greatest concern is not with these theologians but with the church at large. And that "church at large" takes in all varieties of Christians scattered throughout our churches— and all varieties of churches, from fundamentalist to ultraliberal. Thus, all through modern Christendom (even where strict attention is given to maintaining an orthodox theology regarding the biblically specific God), the church nevertheless *performs* primarily as a purveyor of the mysteries of religious peak experience. The churches are every bit as sensitive to their Nielsen ratings as the TV networks are to theirs. If our Christianity were to be tested by how we use it (rather than by what we say about it), we would be found standing foursquare with Maslow: the sole function of religion is to provide its constituents with peak experiences. Like the Nielsen polls, the churches ask one question: "Are our shows appealing—are they giving people the satisfactions (the satisfactions of spiritual experience) they seek?" It is my conviction that the great mass of churchgoers today actually think Christianity exists to no other purpose than to provide them spiritual ecstasy. And the churches are quick to play up to that opinion.

It may be that *churches* think more in terms of a continuity of what might be called "good experience" instead of just exceptional "peaks of experience." And it may be that churches tend more to call it "quality of life"—and thus cherish this good experience not alone for its individual members but also for the faith community as community and even the human race as a society. Yet the Maslowian premise still holds: religion is a phenomenon valued for the sake of what humans see to be their own benefit and enjoyment. Thus, once we look beyond its theological professions and ask *why* a church acts as it does, *what* it is trying to accomplish, it becomes apparent that every form of church "success" (and particularly "church growth") hinges upon one question: Are we providing our people customer satisfaction, what they find to be "good experiences"? Do they come away feeling good about themselves and about the church? Can they then relate their sense of well-being to the well-being of all humanity? Are our religious efforts building toward a situation in which all people can have the peak experience of feeling good about themselves?

This approach to the faith is what John Howard Yoder calls "instrumental." A line from William Henley's familiar poem expresses it well: "I thank whatever gods may be / For my unconquerable soul." The poet's interest in religion—in whatever gods may be—extends only as far as will feed his own sense of "unconquerability." And so often, like Henley, *we* are happy to settle for the mystery of "whatever gods may be" because our one true interest centers sheerly on the peak experience of feeling our souls unconquerable. So don't even ask whether there really is a God or whether our souls actually are unconquerable; as an end in itself, the experiential feeling is everything. It follows that we seek only as much of *God* as can be of instrumental help in pleasing *us*. Indeed, we humans have created religion to no other purpose. And apparently we aren't really open to the idea that things might be exactly the other way around: that God created us to be pleasing to *him*, whether or not we happen to find blessing and have a good experience in the process.

So, no matter how orthodox our professions of the biblically specific God, if it is yet the case that we call upon him—hear and heed him—only insofar as serves our human self-interests, then we are no closer to the gospel than we would be with Maslow's mysterious "maybe-and-maybe-not God," the sheer idea of which will do as much to give us good experience as his actual existence would. In any case, it will bear some thinking about: that the proudly orthodox Christians of the evangelical and conservative churches may be just as guilty of moving God leftward into the realm of inconsequential mystery-experience as are the despised liberals.

Ecclesiastical Mysticism: It is under this heading that we are to look particularly at the sacraments. However, whether regarding the sacraments or any other church-sponsored "worship experience," we are in trouble just as soon as the service stops addressing God (in order to glorify and hallow his name) and becomes more interested in providing meaningful experience for the worshippers (in order to help them feel good about themselves and go forth as better persons). As soon as "religion" takes over with its concern, God is no longer being served as an end in himself (*the* end of all that is) but is himself being used as a means by which humanity serves its own self-interests.

Of course, God does regularly, time and again, offer to serve us in our human need. Yet that always happens in his freedom, at his discretion, and according to what he perceives

to be our need—something quite different from his relin-
quishing the God role to us, that we might use him for our
purposes.

We now center on the sacraments—but we need to make it
quite clear that our critique is addressed not at all to the biblical
institutions of baptism and the Supper but only to Christendom's later "sacramentalizing" of the same. Yet, in truth, the
"sacraments" are well named for what we have made of them;
we use them indeed as "mysterious procedures the church can
perform on behalf of individual believers, thus as much as
guaranteeing God's mysterious response in changing their
spiritual status and transforming them into better persons."
The question, of course, is not whether God can and does
transform people at the time and in the ways of his own choosing. No, the only question is whether the church has been
given the sacramental power to use God, manipulate his mys-
teriousness, and extract peak experiences from him—at the
church's own beck and call.

Quite early in Christian history (as is still the case in large
sectors of the church today), undergoing baptism made it as
much as certain that, as of that moment, the baptized one was
"saved" and guaranteed a place in glory. And that such could
be accomplished through a properly done sprinkle, or bath, of
water—well, that is a great mystery for sure, a matter surpassing all knowledge or comprehension. Quite early in Christian
history (as is still the case in large sectors of the church today),
the Supper was called "the medicine of immortality," the ingesting of which sacramental food had the actual effect of
gradually deifying, divinizing, or immortalizing the one who
partook. "Divine communication" is definitely what was taking
place. And that such could be accomplished through eating a
bit of bread and drinking a sip of wine—well, that is a great
mystery for sure, a matter surpassing all knowledge or comprehension. And it should be said that, customarily, both the
physical accouterments of the service and the liturgy attending
the sacramental practice itself played up the ineffability of the
transpiring mystery. That the sacraments, then, came to bear

the actual name "mysteries" was an entirely predictable occurrence.

Yet even today, when major segments of the church have
massively scaled down and reinterpreted their sacramental
claims regarding baptism and the Supper, the strong note of
mystery remains. The accouterments and the liturgy still
sound the note. The belief still is widely held that, in some
mysterious way, these rites do indeed help one become a better
person and feel good for having been present (and very often
the service is pitched to just this end). And even if, as Maslow
would have it, the rites can be at most an effective means of
inducing peak experiences in those susceptible to them, *that*
variety of mystery is still involved—even to the point of it making no difference whether the biblically specific God actually
exists or not, as long as the worshippers get the religious feelings they covet. Thus, whether interpreted according to a high
sacramentalism or a low one, "sacraments" is still an appropriate name for what we have made of baptism, the Supper, and a
great deal more of Christian worship.

And thus we have the biblical priority pretty well reversed.
Instead of making such "worship aids" our means of coming to
God in order to recognize him for who he is (consequently to
be judged by him, giving ourselves to him that we might be
made conformable to his will and useful in his service), we have
perverted them into aesthetic psychological therapies for promoting the self-affirmation and self-enhancement of self-serv-
ing peak experiences. And notice, too, that all four of the types
of mysticism here described assume that divine communication happens through our *seeking* experience, through our
techniques of "making contact" with the divine, rather than by
letting God take the initiative in contacting *us*.

It needs to be noted that this critique of "sacramentally mysterious worship" in no way desires to eliminate the experiential
component of "emotion/feeling" from the total action of
Christian faith-confession. Kierkegaard, for instance—with
his prominent use of the terms "subjectivity" and "passion"—
was emphatic that this interior side of faith *belongs* and belongs

absolutely. At the same time, however, he was entirely clear about how the feelings must relate to, and what role they must play within, the overall act of faith.

Christian "passion" is the right (and even necessary) *subjective* by-product of a person's full-fledged response to an entirely *objective*, specific, and essentially unmysterious manifestation of God's grace. Of course, the primary (though by no means only) such manifestation was God's giving his Son to die for us. And an objective, public, historical "action of God" of this sort is what, as we shall see, the Fourth Gospel refers to as "the *flesh* of Jesus." Christian passion is quite proper, then—yet only as an integral component of the quite specific and fleshly transaction in which an entirely human-fleshly individual makes a down-to-earth commitment of discipleship in response to God's gracious action in the *flesh* of Jesus (there being nothing mysteriously "spiritual" involved). And in such case, ours is a "passion of thanksgiving" and has significance— not as something that "feels good" to us but simply as a *witness* (and, for us, a *necessary* witness) to the fact that we truly appreciate and feelingly desire to be appropriated by this fleshly manifestation of God's grace.

So neither the Fourth Gospel nor this study has any intention of denigrating Christian passion. As long as it maintains its focus upon and derives its content from the objectivity of God and his fleshly works of grace—and as long as it is valued for God's sake, as a witness to his wonder, majesty, and love— Christian passion is entirely biblical and right. However, just as soon as it trades its focus on the objective "flesh-taking God" for a focus on a subjectivistic "God of mystery"—and as soon as that passion becomes an end in itself, becomes self-interested religious enjoyment—at that point it becomes unbiblical and wrong.

ON GIVING THE BELOVED DISCIPLE HIS SAY

This brings us, finally, to the promised study of the Fourth Gospel, a study intended to demonstrate that the theology of the New Testament essentially prohibits not just sacramentalism but mystery religion in general. Our focus will be the sacraments, but we need also to catch the implications regarding the more inclusive issue of "mystery" per se (which is why we have just reviewed all those other varieties of mystery).

One way of demonstrating the nonsacramental character of New Testament thought is simply by pointing out that the New Testament does not speak sacramentally. The trouble with this, of course, is that it is "an argument from silence." And if you would give it a thought, you would realize that an argument from silence is very difficult to talk about. What can one say? The best I could do is quote the whole of the New Testament and let you note the absence of any positive interest in, or theology of, sacrament and mystery. So, suspecting that neither my publisher nor my readers are ready to put up with that, I am proceeding on my commitment to do a study from simply the Fourth Gospel.

I find it wise to mount this argument in two stages. (I have been told that one has a better chance of success by breaking down one's goal into separate objectives.) I first will argue that the Fourth Gospel (and by implication the rest of the New Testament) will allow no more than *one* sacrament. And then, after I have made that point, I will argue that not even that one should be called a "sacrament."

This study has a history. And, both because some of the people involved deserve credit and because it may be of interest and help to readers, I tell it. Not long ago, in doing research for another book, I discovered that Karl Barth had once said, "There is only *one* sacrament—the one who has himself risen from the dead." (I was curious to know what more he had said on the matter, but that was it.)

A few years before, regarding a different one of my books, I had been in correspondence with Karl Barth's son Markus— himself a professor of New Testament at the University of Basel in Switzerland. In one of his letters to me, quite by chance, Markus enclosed the sheet of his "Five Theses on the Lord's Supper"—and this told me he was working on the Supper.

Quite recently, I happened to enter into correspondence with Arthur Cochrane, an emeritus professor of theology from Dubuque Seminary. And what a unique contact he has turned out to be! First of all, he received at least part of his theological training under Karl Barth and is himself a Barth specialist. Second, he has been a longtime friend and colleague of Markus Barth, serving on the same faculty with him at two different seminaries. And third, Cochrane published his own quite nonsacramental book on the Supper about the same time I published mine (*In Place of Sacraments,* Eerdmans, 1972).

Well, not long ago Cochrane informed me that Markus Barth had just been at Dubuque lecturing on the Supper—the final paper of the series being "Jesus Christ, the One Sacrament (An Exposition of John 6)." That still didn't tell me a whole lot about what under the sun these Barth people were talking about, so Cochrane filled me in with about two sentences more. And it is on the basis of this exhaustive research that I come before you now.

Obviously, then, the present study is entirely my own. My guess is that it will pretty well coincide with (or, perhaps better, "supplement") what Karl Barth, Markus Barth, and Arthur Cochrane have had in mind—but I can't prove that to be the case. So, while I need to credit the Barths with having put me onto the idea, it must be kept clear that the following represents no one's thought other than mine.

As suggested earlier, this study does not depend upon or require much from Study One—except the point that the Beloved Disciple was a well-versed and quite capable philosopher-theologian. For present purposes, the importance of that point is as follows:

Regarding the New Testament position on sacramentalist-mystery thinking, the silence of the Galilean Twelve (i.e., the absence of su⌐h thinking in the Synoptic tradition) surely should be attributed simply to their *ignorance* of the mode of thought, a mode too sophisticated to have come into their ken, a way of thinking that was beyond them and with which they likely had never had much if any contact. The absence of sacramentalist-mystery thinking in the Synoptics is easily explained—at the same time constituting an argument from silence that affords little or no help in the drawing of theological conclusions.

Of course, the Apostle Paul in his time *did* have the requisite background and contacts for being well familiar with mystery thinking—and it is clear that this was indeed the case with him. Nevertheless, Paul's tendency is simply to reject mystery thinking out of hand. He is the biblical writer most insistent that the gospel is essentially a revealer of mystery, a breaker of mystery, rather than a promoter and exploiter of the same. Paul clearly knows mystery thinking in a way the apostolic tradition does not, yet he never fully engages it, credits it, or formulates a careful response to it. He simply dismisses it.

In the New Testament, then, it is the Beloved Disciple who is left to carry the ball—and carry it he does, to one of the most spectacular touchdowns of Scripture. He is intellectually equipped and can do mystery thinking with the best of them—fully capable of addressing either intellectualist Jewish mysticism or any of the philosophic or religious Hellenist varieties. In fact, he is so good at it that, to the present day, the adherents of all our previously listed varieties of Christian mysticism tend to gravitate to the Fourth Gospel for their mystery terminology, for their rationales, for moral support. With its "divine communication," its philosophical conceptualizing of God, its intellectualism, and what all, the Fourth Gospel commonly is read as the most mystical (and sacramental) book of the New Testament—and likewise, the Beloved Disciple as the author most knowledgeable about, appreciative of, and sympathetic toward mystical religion.

All that may very well be true, but it is now my hope to demonstrate that the Beloved Disciple is showing this mystical friendliness deliberately, as a means of setting up these and all other mystics for the kill. As soon as they get within reach, what he is set to do is give them the old straight-arm right under the chin—as he negotiates an end run that whisks the gospel right past them and over the goal line. And it is precisely this straight-arm that right now is giving me procedural difficulty. My first thought had been to build my whole scriptural argument and reveal the straight-arm only at the very end—as the climax, denouement, and hook of the study. Yet presently my opinion is that readers will need to know about the straight-arm in order to see what the Beloved Disciple is about and where his argument is leading. So what I am choosing to do is reveal the secret now—while reserving the right to come back and preach a bit on the subject at the conclusion of the discussion.

The Fourth Gospel Prologue (1:1-18)

Whether or not the Prologue (John 1:1-18) is built over an earlier Hymn to the Logos—this strikes me as an entirely inci-dental question. However, I do think I see what the writer is up to—whether he is reworking a previously existent text or not. I propose that he is working his way along a spectrum from one pole to the other, from LOGOS (the Word) in verse 1 to FLESH in verse 14—"Logos" and "Flesh" being indeed polar opposites. The Logos, for its part, epitomizes that which is most general, abstract, transcendent, ethereal, incomprehen-sible, and mysterious—while the Flesh, for its part, epitomizes that which is most specific, real, mundane, down-to-earth, and concrete. I don't know that the writer could have found any two terms that would better express the polarity.

Readers of Hebrew background likely would have identi-fied the Logos with "the word" by which God originally "spoke" the created universe into being, while readers of Greek per-suasion would have recognized it as a term of divine inter-mediation from out of their own Hellenist philosophies. Yet, doubtless, any educated practitioners of sophisticated religion would have welcomed and promptly clambered aboard this train of thought—which, I suggest, is precisely what the writer wanted them to do. He was getting to his readers by "speaking their language."

The first five verses of the passage present the Logos entirely on the level (and at the pole) of abstract and ideal conceptualizations. What, for instance, might the existence of a *Word* (a Logos) signify when separated from the act of any particular speaker's speaking it? And the text's proceeding to equate the Logos with *Life* and then with *Light* (two of the continuing and pervasive themes of this Gospel, by the way—though never again presented on this level of abstraction)—this is very much to keep things at the pole of intellectualist philosophizing. What, here, might *Life* be when there is no reference to any actual creature's being "alive"? And what might *Light* be when the reference is obviously to something quite different from actual photons? There is nothing in those five verses that can be pinned down, that is in any way specifiable, discernible, or definable. There is no way of testing whether any of it is for real or whether it is all only theological idea and imagining.

I suggest, then, that the writer's first move away from the Logos pole and toward the Flesh pole (and one giant step for Godkind it is) comes in the using of *personal pronouns* for the Logos. Our problem will be in determining just where this switch actually is made. Certainly the nouns themselves (whether "Word," "Life," or "Light") would normally call for the impersonal "it" and as much as prohibit the personal "he" (or "she" even). And there is nothing in these five verses to as much as hint that a personal "he" might be either accurate or appropriate. Moreover, the Greek term in question is itself ambiguous: it can be translated as either a personal "him" or an impersonal "it." So my hunch is that the English translators are wrong in going to the personal pronoun as early as verse 2. I think it would better be held off until verse 10; it's not until that point that there is any contextual justification for understanding the Logos to be a *personal* (a person-like) entity.

That way, the change of pronoun would coincide with the writer's second big move away from the abstraction of Logos and toward the specificity of Flesh. I take it that the verse-9 statement about the true Light's "coming into the world" has reference to a specific, concrete, down-to-earth event in history—is itself a preliminary synonym of the verse-14 Logos becoming Flesh and dwelling among us. I take verse 9 to intend this rather than intending some mysterious, timeless, undetectable action of the Logos by which God is forever percolating his divinity into the human world (as much of modern theology would have it). Either way, though, the next two verses go on to specify that the world summarily *rejected* this coming of the Logos. And from this we must conclude that abstract theories about world divinization are discredited in any case (because the world has not accepted *any* coming of the Logos).

However, I propose a different reading of this reference to the world's resisting the coming of the Logos. By its very nature as "religion," human religiousness of whatever variety welcomes and supports the conceptualizations and thought forms of the Logos pole. "God," "the gods," "ultimate reality," "transcendent being," and the like—all these are fine and dandy (as long as things stay at this level). The Divine is thus kept vague, distant, and nonspecific enough that the human agents retain full control of their "religion." No, it is only when the true Light (which will show up human darkness for what it is) threatens to "come into the world" (i.e., to get specific and down-to-earth)—it is only then that the world (including especially the religious world) quickly decides to know him and receive *him* not.

My particularist reading (rather than the generalist one) is made as much as certain when we see that John 3:16-21 is a post–Logos-became-Flesh statement, the precise parallel of our present passage, the pre–Logos-became-Flesh statement here in John 1:9-13. John 3:17 has God "sending" the *Son* into the world, whereas John 1:9 has the true Logos/Light "coming" into the world—but the idea is the same. Then John 3:19ff. has this *Son* being the light that is "hated," language quite equivalent to that of John 1:10ff., which presents the Logos/Light being "received not." What the author first states *abstractly* about the Logos/Light he proceeds to make *explicit* as a reference to Jesus of Nazareth. I consider it beyond dispute that he recognizes no Logosian enlightenment of the world other than what came (and continues to come) through the flesh of Jesus. And I find no justification at all for the Fourth Gospel's being used (as it long has been used) as a source for abstract, philosophical, generalized theologies. After his initial jump to the Flesh pole, the writer establishes that as his position and never once makes any move back toward Logosian speculation.

The move of the Logos toward becoming Flesh is the most threatening thing that could happen to human religion. When God concretely takes control, the first result is that we humans lose control over our own religion.

With verse 14, then, the writer completes his traversal from LOGOS to FLESH—this in telling us that the Logos (presumably without remainder) has *become* flesh and dwelt among us. And note well, this journey from pole to pole has not been presented as an account of *the writer's* personal theological development. Not at all; he presumes to be speaking as a witness of *God's* own journey and action. It is God who, in historical actuality, has changed himself from Logos to Flesh. The case is not at all that of a theologian changing his personal perception of God.

It follows that the called-for human response must be that of religionists henceforth dropping all their religious efforts to know God *as nondiscrete Logos* and now seeking to know him rather *as that entirely discrete Flesh* which he became to no other purpose than that we might know him in spirit and in truth. The whole religious crew that clambered aboard with the writer's first verse have all jumped ship by the time he gets it to port in verse 14—or, more likely, they have perversely expounded his text to make it agree with their "religious ideas" rather than his "historical claim." Yet it is plain that, in the eyes of the writer, the Logos' becoming Flesh and dwelling among us marks the greatest and most gracious action God has ever taken (and perhaps could ever take) on behalf of humanity.

Now, "flesh" denotes simply specific and concrete historical existence and is not a particular reference to the blood-bearing body tissues that constituted the physical form of Jesus of Nazareth (an idea that shall later be developed in detail). Thus, there is no suggestion that even though Jesus be the incarnate Logos, this "flesh of Jesus" (i.e., his body tissue) was in any way unique. I doubt that an autopsy would have produced any evidence in this regard. However, with Jesus' historical-existence "flesh," the case is just the opposite. So it is here that the incarnation of the Logos is located—in how Jesus historically acted and behaved, in the character of personal existence he demonstrated.

And the writer proceeds to list the unique features that mark this particular Logos-Flesh. The flesh of Jesus, he tells us, is full of "grace," "truth," and "glory" (glory as of "an *only-begotten* of the Father"—just so is the uniqueness emphasized). And the implication simply must be that grace, truth, and glory are things one can never hope to find as natural endowments of normal human flesh (i.e., of customary human historical existence). Thus, as verses 16-17 have it, if ever any hint of these qualities is to be found within (or can be attributed to) normal human flesh, it is because the person involved has picked them up by his flesh having rubbed against the Logos-Flesh of Jesus—it is only through deliberate and intimate contact that this sort of infection spreads. And for sure, an individual with that infection will be the very last to claim it as the glory of his natural humanity—and the very first to claim it, instead, as the grace of God received through none other than the fleshly Jesus of Nazareth.

The writer finally capsulizes and concludes his line of thought with verse 18: "No one has ever seen God; the only Son, who is in the bosom of the Father, he has made him known." That is, no one has ever come to an effective "knowing of God" through specious efforts at mastering the Logos as Logos. No, at that pole, God is entirely beyond us. So, if God is ever to be truly known, it will have to be through the Logos that has become Flesh in Jesus—for that is the only way in which

God has chosen fully to offer himself and make himself accessible to us.

Finally, none of the preceding is to be understood as Vernard Eller's propounding *his* ideas; rather, it is my best effort at letting the Beloved Disciple speak for himself. I hope that those who want to argue will choose to argue with *him*—remembering that he was the contemporary in the best position and best qualified to interpret Jesus.

The Lord's Supper without Sacraments (13:1-30)

With that Prologue straight-arm now revealed, we are ready to work through a careful argument that will time and again bring us right back to John 1:14. As we proceed, our focus will be upon that particular mystery of a sacramental Lord's Supper, though the larger range of mystery thinking will still be constantly in view. So, first, some specific observations about the Beloved Disciple's treatment of the Supper.

The Fourth Gospel has an account of a last supper of Jesus with his disciples precisely where the Synoptics and Paul also have it (the one difference raises a question about whether or not that Thursday evening—although what Jews would know as the first hours of Friday—was also the time of the Jewish Passover meal). Yet, regarding that supper, the Fourth Gospel recounts only the footwashing and a meal (no bread and cup), whereas the other sources recount only the bread and cup with a meal (no footwashing). At the same time, the Fourth Gospel is quite specific in placing the Beloved Disciple in the account as an eyewitness to, and actual participant in, that supper. Obviously, then, the tradition stemming from that Beloved Disciple had to have been fully aware that that supper had also included the actions of the bread and cup. Thus, the Fourth Gospel's omission of the bread and cup must have been *deliberate*—there being no way of explaining it as accident or ignorance.

The question then comes: "Why? Why would the Beloved

Disciple want to leave out of his account the very actions the other witnesses counted as central?" The only answer I can see is that, given the mind-set of the Beloved Disciple against mystery thinking, he was perturbed enough about what he saw as the sacramental misuse of the bread and cup in his day (i.e., toward the end of the first century) that he decided not to include in his Gospel anything that could possibly be used in support of such sacramentalism.

However, it will be at another point of our argument that this omission of the bread and cup becomes crucial. The question will be whether John 6 is meant to refer to the Eucharist. And at least one aspect of the answer will be that it is highly unlikely that an author concerned enough to omit the *referent* (the institution of the bread and cup) would, at another point, make *reference* to what he had deliberately left out.

Then there is another implication to which we should give attention. If, as claimed, the Beloved Disciple was an eyewitness of and actual participant in the supper, then his account of the footwashing establishes that as historical fact just as much as the other accounts establish the bread and cup as such. The *Synoptic* omission of the footwashing no more disproves its having happened than the Fourth Gospel's omission of the Eucharist disproves its having happened. Both actions enjoy equally strong attestation, and the conclusion must be that *both* took place in the upper room. Also, in the Fourth Gospel account, Jesus is reported as saying, "If I then, your Lord and Teacher, have washed your feet, you also ought to wash one another's feet. For I have given you an example, that you also should do as I have done to you" (13:14-15).

In light of the textual evidence, I must admit that I can't begin to follow the churchly logic which says that Jesus instituted the bread and cup as a continuing ritual but not the footwashing, that he established the bread and cup as a "sacrament" but not the footwashing. I fail to see how the two rites can be given any difference of standing at all; I don't see why the case shouldn't be that either we accept both as sacraments or we accept neither as sacraments.

The Woman at the Well (4:1-26)

Now, in pursuit of the idea that Jesus Christ is himself the one sacrament, we go to John 4—as something of a preliminary and warm-up for the main bout of John 6. My feeling is that the Beloved Disciple deliberately structured things this way; in chapter 4 he simply plants the seeds that will come to full flower only in chapter 6.

However, for our purposes, chapter 4 does carry one distinct advantage. Because it is all about the "living *water*," I don't know that anyone has ever tried to argue its having reference to the *sacraments*. The Eucharist, of course, doesn't involve water, and when the talk is all about *drinking* the water, it is difficult even to make it a reference to the *bath* of baptism.

Yet follow the Beloved Disciple's line of thought. A woman of Samaria comes to the well she regularly comes to—this in order to draw the sort of water she regularly draws there. Upon arriving she discovers a man of perfectly normal flesh feeling a very fleshly thirst for the very sort of water she has come to draw. The scene—entirely specific and down-to-earth—is the farthest possible thing from mystery.

In the ensuing conversation, this entirely fleshly man tells her that it would be just as natural for him to satisfy her thirst of spirit by giving her of his water as it would be natural for her to satisfy his physical thirst by giving him of the well water. He says that whoever drinks of his "living water" will never thirst, will have eternal life—and that it is all there for the drinking.

The point, I think, is one with that of the Prologue: all that is needed for our meeting God and coming to know him is the flesh of Jesus (the fleshly Jesus). That's the true way of "divine communication," of worshiping "in spirit and truth" (vv. 23-24). This being so, any attempts to "mysticize" the transaction with the religious paraphernalia of mysterious gnosis, mysterious states of feeling, mysterious priests and sacraments—these are entirely beside the point and completely out of order. True worship is as specific and down-to-earth as drinking water, and has nothing whatever to do with mysteriously proper sacraments administered by proper priests at proper sanctuaries on proper mountains (v. 21).

Yet actually, this account is quite restrained; what is of interest is the number of things the author does not tell us here but will tell us in chapter 6. For instance, here nothing is said about our coming into relation to God—only about receiving eternal life. To which the Beloved Disciple might respond, "Meeting God, receiving eternal life: same difference."

Strangely enough, despite the numerous "I am" statements this Gospel attributes to Jesus, there is no "I am the living water." The closest thing to it is "the water that I shall give," and if Jesus means to be making a distinction between himself and his water, he offers no help as to what it might be. However, later in the Gospel (7:37-39), there is a word strongly reminiscent of the living-water discourse:

"If any one thirst, let him come to me and drink. He who believes in me, as the scripture has said, 'Out of his heart shall flow rivers of living water.'" Now this he said about the Spirit, which those who believed in him were to receive; for as yet the Spirit had not been given, because Jesus was not yet glorified.

Here, identifying "living water" with "the Spirit" solves one problem while creating another. In his offering living water to the woman, Jesus certainly gives the impression that the drinking of it is an immediate possibility for her—not that it must await his glorification and a particular coming of the Spirit. Perhaps the Beloved Disciple's response in this case would be, "Jesus, living water, the Spirit: same difference. State it as you will, it's all one sacrament, not three."

Finally, the living-water discourse does not use the term "flesh," the key word of both the Prologue behind us and chapter 6 ahead. Perhaps the Beloved Disciple would respond, "Use the term 'flesh' or simply portray Jesus in the flesh: same difference." In any case, it seems clear that chapter 4 is a trial run preparing us for the real go of chapter 6—to which there obviously is nothing now to do but go.

Bread—and the Eating of It (6:1-59)

The chapter-six sequence of Jesus first feeding the five thousand, then walking on the water to rescue the disciples, and finally talking to the people after he and the disciples have crossed the lake—this is the only incident (or incident sequence) out of Jesus' Galilean ministry that the Fourth Gospel shares with the Synoptics. Indeed, there is enough coincidence in order of detail and precise wording to suggest that the Beloved Disciple (who makes no claim of having been present) may have taken his account out of one of the Synoptics.

The very real possibility that the bread scene of the feeding followed directly by the water scene of the rescue at sea are meant respectively as references to the Eucharist and to baptism—that symbolic intention is much more likely for the Synoptics than for the Fourth Gospel. Remember that the Fourth Gospel has no Eucharist to serve as referent. Besides, it is clear what the Beloved Disciple is after with his account: he is after the "bread discourse" that forms the major part of his chapter (and of which the Synoptics know nothing). Let's follow the argument he so neatly develops.

Just as chapter 4 opens with an incident involving fleshly people dealing in actual water, chapter 6 opens with an incident of fleshly people dealing in actual bread: Jesus feeds them with bread and fish. A day or so later, following the sea rescue, the crowd catches up to Jesus on the far side of the lake (or the near side, depending upon where you joined the party). There (beginning with verse 25), Jesus talks with them about bread. First he mentions that actual bread: "You seek me, not because you saw signs, but because you ate your fill of the loaves." And he goes on to suggest that this is not a particularly worthy form of seeking him.

Perhaps—just as with his dismissing the woman's first concern for earthly water (which, by the way, is not the same thing as "dirty water")—perhaps Jesus wants to say that any religious yearning by which we seek primarily our own benefit is not true religion. Whether it be the seeking of intellectual satisfaction, mystical ecstasy, peak experience, feeling good about oneself, becoming a better person, quality of life, sociopolitical liberation, triumphant living, the blessing of God, actual water, actual bread—none of these amounts to a seeking of God, who must be sought for his own sake and not as a means of acquiring something for ourselves. "Do not labor for the food which perishes"—including any and all of the above.

The crowd presses Jesus on the point. OK, then, which bread? (This brings us to verse 30.) How about the manna in the wilderness? That must have been pretty good stuff.

Yes, not bad—nor nearly as good as what I have in mind. That was Moses' bread, but I'm talking about God's.

Fine. Give it to us.

"I *am* the bread of life" (v. 35)—which never got said about the living water, though Jesus does go on to specify that, with him, one never ever hungers or *thirsts*.

The hearers do a lot of murmuring at the thought of some plain old no-account human actually being the bread of life. The very idea!

Jesus responds that it has all been the Father's doing and nothing of his own; but, if the Father makes Jesus the bread of life, then he *is* the bread of life. Next he goes one more step: "And the bread which I shall give for the life of the world is my FLESH" (v. 51 and shades of 1:14!).

The Beloved Disciple here goes back to the word "flesh," using it in reference to Jesus for the first time since he introduced it in his Prologue; and after this bread discourse, he will not use it so again. This strategic placement makes it clear that, for the Beloved Disciple, "flesh" is a key concept. So perhaps here is the best place for us to pause and talk about it.

"Flesh," now, obviously cannot refer to the actual body tissues of the man Jesus. To read the Beloved Disciple as suggesting that, in Jesus' case, his body tissues were so different from those of other people that, if eaten, they would have the miraculous effect of making a person immortal—obviously, any such interpretation would put the Beloved Disciple deeply into the very realm of "mystery" he is working so hard to avoid.

Likewise, the Beloved Disciple's word "flesh" deliberately is not Jesus' Last Supper bread word "body"—which Paul subsequently picked up to develop into "the body of Christ." That word "body" needs to be read as "personhood" (*persona,* personal character) so that that character can "characterize" Jesus' corporate following just as well as his individual self. Yet such a reading won't begin to work with the Beloved Disciple's "flesh."

Yet neither will the Beloved Disciple's "flesh" correlate with the Apostle Paul's use of the same word. Paul uses it to identify the weak, creaturely, vulnerable, sin-susceptible side of human nature; the Beloved Disciple obviously does not.

Thus, regarding the Beloved Disciple's unique usage of the word "flesh," I propose that it be taken to identify "the entirely specific and down-to-earth historical existence of that human being known as 'Jesus of Nazareth.'" *Flesh* signifies the very opposite of *Mystery*. And I am now prepared to go Father and Son Barth one better (an opportunity that does not come to a person every day). But the Beloved Disciple is not saying (with them), Jesus Christ is the one sacrament. No, he (with me) is saying, The *flesh* of Jesus is the one sacrament. It will not satisfy the Christian gospel, then, for us to believe in "the mystical Christ," "the spiritual Christ," "the Christ event," "the Christ-spirit," "the world Christ," "the Christ of the sacraments," "the Christ in the poor man," "the Christ who is a *symbol* of this, that, or the other." In fact, my guess is that the Beloved Disciple would protest even "Jesus Christ" if he suspected you were using "Christ" to fog the complete specificity of the fleshliness of Jesus. Yes, Jesus does say that *he* is the bread from heaven, but (in v. 51) he presses on to say that that bread is his FLESH.

Note, then, how he pushes the specificity one step further (in the same verse) when he says of the bread that it is that which "I *shall give* for the life of the world." Yes, the bread is his flesh, yet when he moves on to speak of a future action of "giving" that flesh, he plainly is seeing his death on the cross as the one most specific manifestation of the actuality of his historical existence. It is in the real pain, blood, agony, and death of that occasion that we get our truest insight into Jesus— namely, that he is not some sort of mysterious, spiritual, symbolic divine phenomenon. He is as real a human being as any of us, living in real history, and undergoing just as real a death as any other fleshly person who has ever been executed. So, no more than we dare spiritualize the person of Jesus do we dare spiritualize the cross. It has no meaning unless it be kept real— precisely the opposite of our efforts to give it meaning by spiritualizing it. Yes, Jesus is the bread from heaven (there is no backing off on that), yet he can be "bread" only if he is first recognized as "flesh."

Now, to trace the thread of the discourse again:

"The bread you received yesterday on the other side of lake won't do much for you. You need good bread."

"Fine, but what bread is good bread? The manna in the wilderness?"

"No, even better bread than that. You need the bread that God gives."

"Fine. Show us to it!"

"I am the one truly great bread. Even on manna, those people died. On the bread from heaven, no one need ever die. But, you should know, this bread is my *flesh*."

"You don't say!"

"I do say, and it follows that the only way of getting the bread is by *eating my flesh*."

Jesus elaborates in vv. 53-58:

Truly, truly, I say to you, unless you eat the flesh of the Son of man AND DRINK HIS BLOOD, you have no life in you; he who eats my flesh AND DRINKS MY BLOOD has eternal life, and I will raise him up at the last day. For my flesh is food indeed, AND MY BLOOD IS DRINK INDEED. He who eats my flesh AND DRINKS MY BLOOD abides in me, and I in him. As the living Father sent me, and I live because of the Father, so he who eats me will live because of me. This is the bread which came down from heaven, not such as the fathers ate and died; he who eats this bread will live for ever.

[End of the Discourse Proper]

The four "blood phrases" marked out in capital letters are really going to give us fits. So, for the nonce, let's simply ignore them and complete our exposition.

The Beloved Disciple's bread discourse comes out just where logic would say it should. Once informed that the bread of life is indeed the flesh of Jesus, what is one supposed to do about it? Regarding bread, obviously it accomplishes nothing simply to think about it, to speculate about it, to do a chemical analysis of it or look for the recipe, to affirm that it is real, to comment on it, preach about it, adore it, or even thank God for it. (Of course, *after* one has eaten the bread, any of these activities might be proper—yet none can begin to *take the place of* eating it.) With bread there is only one thing to do—and that is *eat* it. There is no point at all in God's giving the bread from heaven in the form of the flesh of Jesus unless someone is willing to eat it. "Divine communication" hasn't happened until we are as ready to "eat" as God is to "give."

In fact, the Beloved Disciple's chosen Greek word at that point, rather than "eat," would better be translated "masticate"—as honest, direct, and down-to-earth a word as can be found. It is the Concordant Literal New Testament that contributes the translation "masticate." Strong's Concordance says that the Greek word may have reference to the sound of *crunching* and might be translated "gnaw" or "chew." (And let not anyone pretend to be offended at the Beloved Disciple's having Jesus talk that way. We do it all the time in English: "That sermon really gave me some food for thought; I'll have to chew on it for a while, though I trust I'll get it digested.") But the point is that our appropriation of Jesus is to be just as earthly-specific as was the Logos's initial becoming flesh. There dare be no more mystification of our response than there was of his approach: "If I have condescended to come to you as FLESH, then you had better have yourselves ready to CHEW."

So what does the Scripture have in mind, virtually ordering us to chomp down on the flesh of Jesus? Well, Arthur Cochrane reports that Markus Barth said in his lecture, "To eat is to believe, and to believe is to eat." Afterward, Cochrane had to inform Barth that, although it was a good line, Martin Luther had said it first. (Markus Barth now informs me that it was Saint Augustine who said it first. So please guard against giving Luther any credit in this connection.) However, in the present case Luther (or Augustine) was not speaking simply out of his magnificent obsession; he had the textual evidence to back it up. Although it wasn't pointed out previously, the word "believe" appears six different times in the bread discourse (in vv. 29, 30, 35, 36, 40, 47). Luther (or Augustine)—and Barth—and Cochrane—are right.

Yet there is another point to be made here. At these junctures Jesus makes it clear that it is those who "believe" who receive life from their eating. Yet, in a couple other places (vv. 37-40 & 44) he has it that it is only those whom the Father has "given him," or "drawn to him," who receive. And it strikes me that the only way to keep the two ideas from contradicting each other is to understand that "faith" is not at all a good work we produce out of ourselves (from our side) but is itself a work of God (from his side), a giving to us—or, if you will, a drawing of us to him. Nevertheless, where the Beloved Disciple beats out Luther and everyone else is in his insistence that the very concept "faith" dare not be allowed to become vague, ethereal, and spiritual—that is, to identify just any sort of nonspecific believing something about something or other (belief in general). No, believing faith has to be as direct, concrete, and content-specific as a real person's drinking real water or chomping real flesh. No real person can simply "drink"; he can only drink *something* (and a something capable of quite precise definition).

And just so, believing in anything other than that one "flesh of Jesus" is to be eating junk food that doesn't have enough substance to provide even a good chew.

Outside the bread discourse, the Beloved Disciple speaks two different times of our relation to God through Jesus in ways that go even beyond "faith"—though I would prefer to understand them instead as dimensions of faith that go beyond what the bread discourse has told us.

The first passage is 12:26: "If any one serves me, he must follow me; and where I am, there shall my servant be also; if any one serves me, the Father will honor him." It is by serving, obeying, and following him that one is *with* Jesus, and if you are with Jesus, then you are where he is—namely, with the Father. And I think the Beloved Disciple would say that this is the *only* way to be with God, the only true method of "divine communication." Mystical and sacramental methods won't do. So let us now revise Luther's statement to read, To eat is to believe in such a way as to serve, obey, and follow Jesus. And the final step, then, comes with 17:20-23 (still speaking of divine communication):

I do not pray for these only, but also for those who believe in me through their word, that they may all be one; even as thou, Father, art in me, and I in thee, that they also may be in us, so that the world may believe that thou hast sent me. The glory which thou hast given me I have given to them, that they may be one even as we are one, I in them and thou in me, that they may become perfectly one, so that the world may know that thou hast sent me and hast loved them even as thou hast loved me.

The logic here is clear. Because (as incarnate Logos) Jesus is already one with the Father, anyone who becomes one with Jesus also becomes one with his fellow believers and one with the Father at the same time. Through Jesus, all become one. The logic is clear, yet, when we forget that the passage comes from the particular Gospel which specifies that the *Logos* became FLESH, our application becomes the fuzziest of all. The passage most often is used as referring to some sort of mystical unity of humanity as a whole—quite without regard for any fleshly Jesus. Yet even the ecclesiastical reading regularly has the passage speaking of a mystical church coming into mystical union with a mystical God through the mystical offices of a mystical Christ—without a shred of flesh anywhere to be seen.

But it won't wash. The passage comes from the Gospel of the Beloved Disciple, and his Jesus never talks "fuzzy." No, becoming one with Jesus must take place through our masticating his flesh. Becoming one with Jesus (and thus coming into divine communication with God) can happen only through one's forming a very concrete and specific union with the man Jesus of Nazareth—a union as focused and specific as a particular man's covenanting with a particular woman to become one flesh with her. Mystical unions (i.e., spiritual marriages with "womanhood in general") just won't do, and we must finally revise Luther's statement to read thus: To eat is to believe in such a way that we serve, obey, and follow Jesus to the point of becoming covenantally united with him (what Paul would call "a communion in the body of Christ"). But no mysterious spiritualities are involved.

There can be no becoming one *by means of* hocus-pocus (a term presumed to have been derived from the bread word of the Latin mass). And there can be no becoming one *apart from* actual fleshly discipleship. "The Bread of Life"? Make it as mystical as you wish; there is still no getting around the fact that this bread is "my FLESH."

Is It "Bread" or "Bread and Cup"?

That is my exposition of the bread discourse. But we still need to go back and contend with the "drink my blood" phrases of verses 53-56. I would be just as happy not to, but what scholarship says must be done we dare not fail to do.

The question raised by that passage is whether it refers to

the Eucharist. Many students have said "yes." On the other side, my informant Arthur Cochrane says this: Despite the fact that, on other grounds, Martin Luther developed and taught a highly "sacramental" view of the Supper, he was of the opinion that John 6 includes no reference to the bread and cup. Subsequently, Chief Justice Luther has been supported in this decree by Justices Karl Barth, Markus Barth, Arthur Cochrane, and now Vernard Eller. That is pretty impressive, I admit—but there may still be doubters who insist on examining the evidence. I quote it once more, so that we can have the record before us (John 6:53-56):

Truly, truly, I say to you, unless you eat the flesh of the Son of man AND DRINK HIS BLOOD, you have no life in you; he who eats my flesh AND DRINKS MY BLOOD has eternal life, and I will raise him up at the last day. For my flesh is food indeed, AND MY BLOOD IS DRINK INDEED. He who eats my flesh AND DRINKS MY BLOOD abides in me, and I in him.

Allow me to make several points about the passage:

(1) In my earlier book—*In Place of Sacraments* (pp. 80-84)—I found this passage (as a passage) creating real difficulty. Now I see that such is not the case at all. The interpretation here has been that, given Jesus' *being* the bread, the discourse as much as *has* to move to a conclusion regarding our *eating* it. And as we also have seen, "masticating Jesus' flesh" is, for the Beloved Disciple, exactly the right way of putting the matter. The problem is not at all with the "passage" but simply with those four "blood phrases."

(2) If—*if*—in its account of the Last Supper the Fourth Gospel included anything close to the drinking of blood, then we would be hard put to deny that at least these four verses seem to imply a reference to the Eucharist. *However,* because in point of fact the Fourth Gospel includes no eucharistic account of any sort, the logic runs the other way—*against* the likelihood that the passage refers to something that isn't there.

(3) The blood language of these verses is definitely an *intrusion*. Right up until this passage (through v. 52) the language has all been about "eating"—eating bread (or eating the flesh that we explicitly have been told the bread is). Then come four verses which—completely out of the blue—insist on adding "drinking" (and the drinking of "blood," even). Yet, with the verse immediately following (v. 57), we are back to the single theme of "eating"—with no mention of drinking, or the drinking of blood, ever being made again.

(4) The controlling metaphor of the entire discourse is, obviously, the bread of life as the new *manna*. The manna is mentioned as close as three verses ahead of the problem language and in the second verse following it. Yet those references to "drinking blood" blow the metaphor completely; there is nothing in the "manna picture" that begins to correspond with drinking blood.

(5) If the Beloved Disciple deliberately included these references to blood in his crucial discourse, he utterly failed to give his readers any help in understanding what he intends by them. Nowhere in the Fourth Gospel other than here does the writer even use the word "blood" (except for two passing references, only one of which might even possibly include theological overtones). But other than here, the Beloved Disciple never gives us as much as a hint of the wider biblical imagery involving blood: there is never any talk about "the blood of covenant," "the blood of sacrifice," "washed in the blood," "saved by the blood," "this cup is my blood," or anything of the sort. The Beloved Disciple does, of course, speak long and frequently about "life"—yet he never makes "blood" a graphic symbol of it, as so many of the other biblical writers do. If we might put it so, the Fourth Gospel—with its lack of any account of the Eucharist and with the exception of this four-phrase intrusion—is about the most bloodless book of the New Testament. So how were we meant to understand this unsignaled and unexplained reference to the drinking of blood?

(6) This sudden reference is also problematic from another

standpoint. The discourse (which, recall, was recorded by one who was likely a Jewish rabbi) is firmly attached to a *Jewish* setting: a Jewish Jesus (as rabbi) is speaking to a Jewish audience in a Jewish synagogue about the Jewish story of manna in the wilderness. *Yet* in this situation every person present would have known absolutely that the very law of God absolutely prohibits any drinking of blood. If, in this setting, Jesus had simply thrown into his discourse some side remarks concerning the drinking of blood—even that could not have gone without notice. At the very least, there would have been angry demands for an explanation and, most probably, a riot. My own hunch is that the sacramental idea of "drinking blood" could not have come into Christian tradition until comparatively late, after the members of the church were mostly non-Jewish—namely, people of pagan background for whom "blood drinking" would make perfectly good (religious-sacramental) sense. And the most probable reading of Jesus' upper-room cup word is "This cup is the new covenant in my blood"—and not "This cup is my blood."

(7) Inevitably, the first effect of introducing "drink my blood" is to call into question our understanding of "chew my flesh." There is no problem, of course, in a writer's varying his imagery in presenting what is actually one idea—as the Beloved Disciple himself has done in making "drinking the living water" (chapter 4) the equivalent of "eating the bread of life" (chapter 6). No confusion there. Yet, to put "drink my blood" *in tandem with* "chew my flesh" is an entirely different matter. If the two phrases are meant to be redundant, each conveying the very same idea, then what have the "blood phrases" accomplished except to confuse people? If, on the other hand, "drink my blood" is meant to convey something different from "chew my flesh," what is that difference? The author certainly doesn't tell us, and the likelihood is that we would be forced to go back and completely redefine "flesh" in the process of finding a "flesh" idea and a "blood" idea that would make sense in tandem.

(8) Plainly, the Beloved Disciple was a very careful thinker and writer. If he *wanted* this bread discourse to refer to the Eucharist, he could have found a much better and clearer way of doing it than simply by attaching four "blood phrases." And conversely, if he *didn't* want to refer to the Eucharist, he could have left out those "blood phrases"—and no one ever would have had much grounds for arguing that John 6 does refer to the Eucharist.

(9) We need to recognize that, in the original Greek, these four phrases are just as independent and expendable as they are here in the English. That is, any one of them or all of them can be either included or omitted without in any way changing the sentence structure of the passage. (Because the Greek original didn't have punctuation, it wouldn't be necessary to change even that much.) And it is my opinion that the phrases can be included or omitted without changing the *sense* of the passage, either; it says the same thing whether they be in or out. The only difference is that, with the blood phrases in, the passage could conceivably be referring to the Eucharist.

So, except for the fact of their presence in the text, I find no indication that the Beloved Disciple would have written these phrases or even wanted them in. Then what possible explanation is there? Well, consider that if, somewhere down the line, the Gospel had as copyist a dedicated sacramentalist who really felt the discourse must have been intended to support his own understanding of the Eucharist—well, then, the addition of four simple phrases would assist wonderfully. According to his lights, the copyist would not be "changing" the Gospel but only "clarifying" it. (And don't say such a thing couldn't happen; the Living Bible "paraphrase" does this with some regularity.)

[Only after it was too late to do anything about it—except this—I learned that the foregoing requires radical correction. Markus Barth has informed me that my "fits" over the blood language were both unnecessary and uncalled for. The phrase "eat my body *and drink my blood*" can and does make perfectly good sense—without at all slipping into reference to the Eucharist. (1) "Flesh and blood" can be a normal way of referring to a human totality—as this writer himself does in John 1:13 (cf. Matt. 16:17; 1 Cor. 15:50; Eph. 6:12; Heb. 2:14). However, much more important, (2) we noted that the close-by reference of John 6:51 related the living bread to Jesus' giving his life for the world—which specifies, of course, his blood-spilling crucifixion. The author wants to call us to more than just an "eating it down" quality of faith in the *fleshly* Jesus (i.e., his incarnation as a truly human individual); the author wants to call us more particularly to a faith in that fleshly Jesus who *shed his blood* for us. So, along with a "chewing" faith in his *flesh* belongs a "drinking" faith in his *blood*. Yet be clear that, for this writer, the blood he would have us drink is that of the cross—not of any communion table (and so does not flout any Jewish scruples about actually ingesting blood).

So, for an authoritative exegesis of the matter, don't look to *this* book; rather, read Markus Barth, *Rediscovering the Lord's Supper* (John Knox, forthcoming).]

Chapters One, Four, Six—and Beyond

Beyond the "demystification of the gospel" that we now have found in the Prologue, in the living-water discourse, and in the bread-of-life discourse, the Fourth Gospel includes some scattered passages which have the effect of confirming that reading.

"If you knew me, you would know my Father also" (8:19). Jesus again is specified as the one way to (the one divine communication of) the Father, although in this instance his "fleshliness" is not insisted upon.

"I and the Father are one" (10:30)—and of the two, of course, it is the fleshly Jesus who is our access to the heavenly Father (rather than vice versa).

"He who believes in me, believes not in me but in him who sent me. And he who sees me sees him who sent me" (12:44-45). In other words, quit trying, through means of mystery, to enter into divine communication with the God of Mystery. Just *look* at the fleshly Jesus and *see* the heavenly Father—and that's as much of "God" as you ever *need* to know, *can* know, or should even *want* to know.

"I am the way, and the truth, and the life; no one comes to the Father, but by me. If you had known me, you would have known my Father also; henceforth you know him and have seen him" (14:6-7). Though I have no desire to reject the broader interpretation of this saying, my guess is that it originally had a somewhat different application from what we normally give it. Jesus, recall, is talking to his disciples (those who are already Christian believers) and so does not likely have foremost in mind all those nonbelievers who must, if ever, come to the Father by him. Rather, for those who already claim Christ, the word would seem to be, "Sorry, but it is not your prerogative to define 'Christ.' It was never said that the Mystic Christ, the Sacramental Christ, the Christ of Gnosis, the Spiritual Christ, the Christ of Personal Preference could get you to the Father. No one comes to the Father but by the one, specific, down-to-earth *me*."

"He who has seen me has seen the Father; how can you say, 'Show us the Father'?" (14:9). And how can we, apparently having learned nothing from Jesus' rebuke of Philip, for two thousand years now keep on saying, "Show us the Father"?— and not just keep on *saying* it, but keep trying to see God through every religious invention in the book, only to keep winding up with nothing more than psychological peak experiences that (Maslow says) could as well be induced through drugs, music, or sex.

"Yet a little while, and the world will see me no more, but you will see me" (14:19). Here is a problem we have not addressed but ought to: How is it possible for us latter-day Christians to chomp the flesh of Jesus when that flesh is no longer dwelling among us? At that point, do we have any choice except to go to a more "spiritual" relationship?

Jesus says that his presumed absence is indeed a problem for the world but not for Christians. And be reminded that, there in the Fourth Gospel, in his insistence about our chewing the flesh, the Beloved Disciple was himself addressing readers for whom the literal flesh of Jesus was already as absent as it is for us now. Obviously, neither Jesus nor the Beloved Disciple ever meant to say that only the earthly contemporaries of the historical Jesus had the possibility of knowing him in the flesh.

So, I suggest, we are here being given divine counsel about how our approach to God (or our response to God's approach) must proceed. If we are to have any hope of seeing God, we must go first to the New Testament (and particularly, the Beloved Disciple would want me to say, to the Fourth Gospel that he produced for the very purpose: "These are written that you may believe that Jesus is the Christ, the Son of God, and that believing you may have life in his name"—20:31). There we must learn just as much as we can about who this Jesus of Nazareth was, how he acted, what he taught, and what sort of person he was in his historical actuality. Then, the Beloved Disciple continues, those who, out of this knowledge of Jesus' flesh, believe in such a way that they serve, follow, and obey Jesus to the point of being covenantally united as one flesh with him—those people are "chomping the flesh," "eating the bread of life," and "seeing God."

But the one conclusion regarding Jesus' leave-taking that the Beloved Disciple will not allow is the one we are most prone to draw: if the flesh is gone, that must make our relationship to Christ *spiritual*—the spiritual way of sacrament, inner experience, religious enlightenment, and what all. To which the Beloved Disciple has Jesus respond, "True, the world will see me no more, but *you* will *see me*. And when I say 'see,' I mean see the real me, see me in the flesh. So start chewing that one flesh which, now as then, is food indeed."

An Assist from Søren Kierkegaard

It was only upon writing to this point that I suddenly remembered that all this is just what Kierkegaard was after by insisting that true Christian faith consists solely in "contemporaneousness with Christ." Of that concept, Kierkegaard himself said,

This is the decisive thought! This thought is the central thought of my life. And I may say too with truth that I have had the honor of suffering for bringing this truth to light. Therefore I die gladly, with infinite gratitude to Governance that to me it was granted to be aware of this thought and to make others attentive to it. Not that I have discovered it. God forbid that I should be guilty of such presumption. No, the discovery is an old one, it is that of the New Testament. (*Attack upon Christendom,* p. 242)

That statement falls short only in failing to give specific credit to the Beloved Disciple. And it could be that, even though he never got it said in so many words, Kierkegaard was ahead of the Barths in understanding Jesus Christ as the one sacrament. For a full exposition of Kierkegaard's concept of "contemporaneousness," consult my first book, *Kierkegaard and Radical Discipleship* (Princeton University Press, 1968), pp. 356-83. And then, for Kierkegaard's few but relevant words on "sacramentalism," see pp. 325-28.

In a nutshell, Kierkegaard's "contemporaneousness" says something of this sort: Through a deliberate action of mind and will, you do your best to put yourself into the same relation to the historical Jesus which necessarily would have been that of the Beloved Disciple and Jesus' other contemporaries, both those who ultimately chose to believe and those who chose not to. That is, you try to face Jesus as being a real, live, fleshly individual no different from anyone else—who nevertheless says some things and does some things hinting that he is acting as far more than just a normal human being.

And remember that these hints will make your situation harder rather than easier. For every thing you see indicating that Jesus might actually be the Logos become flesh, you will see hundreds of indications that he is only a peasant preacher from Galilee. So, regarding this most problematic man of flesh, you make your own decision—making it in the context of that real and difficult specificity rather than in the easy context of simply accepting whatever mysterious dogma the church tells you it knows for certain about a spiritual presence of Jesus.

Or, in the terminology of the Beloved Disciple, when that completely unexceptional Galilean peasant tells you he is the bread of life and that the bread is his *flesh*, you be ready to chew like mad—even if that flesh proves tough and undigestible, carrying the flavor of contradiction, scandal, suffering, trauma, and arduousness that is not quite what you had in mind as a satisfying religious experience. You eat it because it is what God has put before you, not because you find it to your liking.

The Flesh as a Communications Unscrambler

Let it once more be said that neither Kierkegaard nor the Beloved Disciple here (nor anyone cited elsewhere in this book) has any desire to use faith's focus upon the *objective* "flesh of Jesus" as a ploy for eliminating, denying, or belittling the *subjective* and experiential side of faith. The issue, rather, is that of *priority*. Let me, then, try putting the *idea* of the Beloved Disciple's "Bread of Life" Jesus into the *mouth* of the Synoptic "Sermon on the Mount" Jesus:

"Be not anxious to *seek* the personal spiritual satisfactions of self-indulgent peak experience. What is to be *sought* is none of these things that your heavenly Father already knows you need (and is perfectly capable of granting). No, *seek* first the objective, other-oriented, self-denying action of masticating that flesh which (whether you like it or not) God has put before you—and whatever you need in the way of spiritual experience will be added to you as well."

This order of priorities is the only workable one—because the objective norm of "the flesh of Jesus" is absolutely essential to the sorting out of our subjective experience. We are following up on Kierkegaard's concept of *subjectivity*, then, in suggesting that a believer's "Christian experience" is to be understood as the impingement of an *objective*, wholly-other deity upon his *inner consciousness*. Thus, for example, the action of an objective (i.e., an altogether "not-me") Holy Spirit arouses certain sensations and feelings that nevertheless exist altogether "within me." " 'Things beyond our seeing, things beyond our hearing, things beyond our imagining, all prepared by God for those who love him,' these it is that God has revealed to us through the Spirit" (1 Cor. 2:9-10, NEB). Yet, pray tell, just how are we supposed to distinguish these "beyond" things from those things that in fact are "from" *our* seeing, from *our* hearing, from our very own imagining?

The *experience* of these things is totally *subjectivistic*. So how am I (either "I" individually or "I" as the "we" of our common cultural subjectivism) to sort out those that are "of God" from those that are of purely human psychology, that are of our cultural background, that are of my genetic makeup, that are of my imagination, that are of Satan, that are of my just having had a good meal?

Most often, I propose, we do this sorting on the grounds of pure *subjectivism*. We have nothing of a "beyond ourselves" to use as an objective point of reference, and so we proceed to operate very much on the basis of our own individual and cultural imaginings. I identify as "of God" whatever experiences feel to me like what I imagine "of God" experiences ought to feel like. What to me *feels* "real good" is what I have in mind when I judge something to *be* real good. God, of course, is something real good. (Possibly, even, "God" is nothing other than the *name* I give to whatever I find to be real good—and what is thus my "ultimate concern.") In any case, that which makes me feel real good becomes the only possible standard for my identifying which are my "of God" experiences.

Yet, in this situation of pure subjectivism, I myself actually am functioning as the only true "God" involved. I am the one Authority, the one Lord, who has full say about what understanding of God, of his Good, and of my good experience shall be attributed to deity. There is no objective, beyond-myself norm by which my identification of God can be gauged as either true or false, right or wrong. I'm the one to say who or what my God is—and of course, *my* God is all of God I can ever experience or know.

Yet the Fourth Gospel claims to have a solution (the only possible solution) to this dilemma of religious subjectivism. "Christian subjectiv*ity*" (as is never the case with pure "subjectiv*ism*") always includes an objective norm that is objectively accessible to us: "No one comes to the Father but by *me*." It is not that Christian experience is always *limited to* but that it must ever and always *start with* and *proceed from* God's objective revelation of himself in "the flesh of Jesus."

So, how do I go about sorting out which of my experiences truly are "of God"? Well, the Fourth Gospel says that I begin by masticating the flesh of Jesus—and that provides me the wherewithal for making the test: Whatever of human experience arises from (or leads to) *faith* in Jesus as the incarnate Logos of divine communication and which then comports with that *flesh*, manifesting the character of that which, in him, was seen *in the flesh*—whatever experience passes this test can be taken as being "of God." With anything else—no matter how right and good I subjectivistically feel it to be—I can never be confident I'm getting a true reading. Indeed, I think this "litmus test of the flesh" is what Scripture means when it tells us to "test the spirits to see whether they are of God" (1 John 4:1).

Accordingly, if, in your experience of Christ's spiritual presence, your walk with the living Lord, your being with Jesus—if in all this you have never found his presence indicating anything other than his being near to comfort and cheer (to affirm you as a "person," to minister to your personal needs, to serve your mental health, spiritual growth, moral development, and sense of social responsibility), then that would seem to raise a serious question about whether your "Jesus of experience" has passed the flesh test. All the New Testament witnesses say that the objective norm of the fleshly Jesus has him much more representative also of "costly grace"—of judging our falsity and calling us to confession and repentance, of bringing not peace but a sword, of commanding us to follow him in radical discipleship, of asking us to deny ourselves and take up our cross daily.

Thus, the objective "flesh test" serves to keep our subjectivistic biases from taking control of God. It gives us a means of sorting out true deity from our own religious imaginings of the same. And it ensures that what we claim to be "of God" actually is "of God." The *flesh* of Jesus must always take precedence over our *spiritual* experiences of him and thus of God. As the Beloved Disciple put it, right off the bat in his Prologue: "No one has ever seen [let alone been given any hold upon] God; the only Son, . . . he has made him known."

(This line of thought, I propose, also takes care of the long-debated theological disagreement about Karl Barth's deep opposition to anything that could be called "natural theology." I submit that Barth was never even addressing the rather theoretical question about just how much of communication with God might be possible through means other than that of his incarnation in Jesus Christ. No matter how much of that communication you might claim could take place outside of Christ, Barth wouldn't argue. He was saying nothing more than that, without the "flesh test of contemporaneousness," we have no way of determining whether or not we are truly in communication with God. With it, of course, we can distinguish all sorts of true communication happening all over the place. If you will, the flesh of Jesus serves as the communications "unscrambler" that suppresses the human static, decodes the true signals of God, and allows them to be formed into a coherent picture for us. And for Barth, then, "natural theology" identified simply any religious system proposing to operate without an "unscrambler." And I, for one, am convinced that Barth has Kierkegaard, the Beloved Disciple, and for that matter, the whole of the Christian gospel on his side.)

An Assist from Martin Buber, Too

By establishing the flesh of Jesus as the one necessity of divine communication, I understand us to be agreeing with what the Barths mean in speaking of "Jesus Christ, the one sacrament." And, in effect, what that says is this: If we are to have any sacrament at all, it cannot be the mysterious, spiritual, symbolic, and altogether unfleshly rituals we have chosen to call "sacraments." If the Christian gospel knows anything of "sacrament," it can be nothing other than this one flesh of Jesus.

However, I think the Barths would agree that—even if Jesus is the one—"sacrament" is probably our poorest possible choice as the noun identifying *what* he is. We have seen that the Beloved Disciple's word "flesh" (meaning "the entirely specific earthliness of historical existence") is as much as the diametric opposite of our word "sacrament" (with its inevitable overtones of mystery, spirituality, and unearthliness). Thus, "the flesh of Jesus is the one sacrament" is as much as a contradiction in terms. (Be clear that I am not at all arguing with the Barths—only seeking the most precise way for expressing our idea.)

So, if "sacrament" doesn't say it, can I propose a word that will? I can. It is the biblical-Hebrew word HOLY. "The flesh of Jesus is the one true Holy." However, I must be quick to insist that this word "holy" be understood in none other than its biblical sense—and not at all in our common religious sense, which simply throws it in with "sacrament," "mystery," "ineffable," "mystical," and all the rest. There is a difference—a big difference—and that difference has perhaps best been explained by the Jewish Hebrew-language scholar Martin Buber. His commentary upon Isaiah's call-vision in the temple is the occasion for his explaining the biblical concept of "holy":

The word "holy" is a concept which cannot be understood unless its definition is followed by a limitation. Up to the Babylonian exile "holy" means distinct but not severed, distinct and yet in the midst of the people ("a holy one in thy midst" Hos. 11, 9); distinct and radiating. . . . YHVH [Yahweh] is absolute master of the world because although He is definitely distinct from the world, He is not in any way withdrawn from it. And for this very reason this conception makes possible a new and the highest expression of the demand to imitate God: that Israel should be holy, as their God is holy. . . . That YHVH is present to Israel even with . . . His holiness, and that Israel is thereby able to receive His influence to follow His footsteps . . . in other words, the hallowing of Israel by the holy YHVH [cf. Ex. 31, 13], this is the root idea of the divine attribute so dear to Isaiah. (*The Prophetic Faith*, pp. 128-29)

The holy God (the *Logos,* if you will) *would* be Mystery to us—except for the fact that his being "holy" means also that his "differentness" is manifested and made accessible to us "in the flesh." And just so, our only way of meeting God and having his holiness communicated into our lives is through this fleshly, in-our-midst manifestation.

Goodness gracious, the Beloved Disciple turns out to be not nearly as original a thinker as we had thought. All in the world he has done is expound the Christian gospel in terms of his ancient Jewish concept of God's *holiness.* And with his having done so, I propose we are completely justified in revising the Barthian formula to read thus: The flesh of Jesus is the one true Holy. The gospel has no need for as much as the word "sacrament"—not even in reference to that "only one" which Jesus really is.